TOMBSTONE INSCRIPTIONS OF KING GEORGE COUNTY, VIRGINIA

By Margaret C. Klein

CLEARFIELD COMPANY

Reprinted for
Clearfield Company, Inc., by
Genealogical Publishing Co., Inc.
Baltimore, Maryland
1994

Dedicated to

my granddaughter

XAN KLEIN

who at age two was my constant companion

and biggest booster

INTRODUCTION

In the spring of 1978 we purchased Tom Lee's General Store, which was known as SHILOH. It had an interesting history, and from the court records we were able to trace the ownership of the property, including the store, to 1811.

We decided one good way to get acquainted with a county, its backroads, its homes both large and small, and the people was by locating all of the family cemeteries we could. We had recently enjoyed such a project in Orange County, Virginia and found it a good activity. We have had a long term interest in genealogy and wanted to "leave behind" something that would contribute in a positive way to the genealogists of the future. A second reason for our interest was that there was so little in the local library, in the state library or in the DAR library on King George County and its importance in the growth of the United States.

Toward the end of the summer we came upon a manuscript written in 1962 by Hugh Roy Stuart. It was a loving story of his associations in King George County, with many references to various family cemeteries. That manuscript, together with a USGS topographical map series and a county road map, set us on our way. We began to pursue the cemeteries of King George County in earnest.

It was our policy to get permission to visit from the present property owners, or at least from someone working on the property. This necessitated many repeat visits. It was well worth the trouble. We had so many pleasant experiences and met so many lovely people, it would be unfair to name some and omit others.

We do offer our thanks here to those who so graciously opened not only their cemeteries, but their homes, their family Bibles, and their personal knowledge of the county. They were each and every one wonderful in their own way.

Our thanks go to the funeral directors of the area. They were fantastic in their willingness to give us help. One kind gentleman put us in his car and drove us up one road and down another pointing out a dozen cemeteries within a mile of his place of business. He then introduced us to an "oldtimer" who also provided more information.

We talked to storekeepers, post office persons, hunters, farmers, to everyone we thought could help us. We tried to make this a comprehensive book of those tombstone inscriptions of persons who either died before 1900 or were born before 1850. We included wives or husbands and occasionally children who did not fit our criteria, but whom it seemed appropriate to include.

Of course, in the family cemeteries we included every headstone. We also noted any information we could glean from owners, neighbors, or others.

The church and proprietary cemeteries will be cared for and will exist for years to come. Many of the small family plots are already deteriorating from weather and lack of care. Perhaps this book will in some small way help preserve the eighty or so we found. A search through county records might reveal many other recorded cemeteries, but without a good guide, finding them would be a task of years. We hope those of you who do know of or have small family cemeteries on your property will eventually copy them and make them available for a supplement to this book when enough have been recorded.

We hope errors in typing and recording are at a minimum. We often seem to work under difficulties. The cemeteries, for the most part, were clean and rather easy to record, but some required rubbings, others scrambling through poison ivy. Evidence of neglect generally indicated the family had died out or moved away. New owners give a right of way to care for and visit family cemeteries. They do not necessarily promise to care for them.

This book contains two indexes: one of names of those who are mentioned in the body of the book and a shorter index of places, which points up the close links between Maryland, just across the Potomac, and King George County. Some of the cemeteries we knew were located near the water can no longer be reached, as no roads exist. Look at a map as you search through this book and you will quickly visualize how the rivers served as highways in the earliest days of King George County, Virginia.

1 March 1979
Locust Grove, Virginia   M.C.K.

TABLE OF CONTENTS

INTRODUCTION   v

MEMORIALS
To Officers and Soldiers of the Confederate Army   1
To Those Who Served in World War   1

PROPRIETARY CEMETERIES
Historyland Memorial Park   2
Oakland Cemetery   2
Peace and Light Cemetery   2
Private Fenced Cemetery near Fletcher's Chapel   3
Private Unfenced Cemetery near Fletcher's Chapel   3
Sharp Hill Cemetery   3

CHURCH CEMETERIES
Antioch Baptist   4
Emmanuel Episcopal   4
First Baptist Church of Ambar   5
Fletcher's Chapel United Methodist Church Cemetery   5
Full Gospel Revival Center   7
Good Hope Baptist Church at Ninde   7
Grace Methodist   7
Hanover Baptist   8
Lamb's Creek Church   9
Little Ark Baptist [new section]   9
Little Ark Baptist [old section]   9
Montague Baptist   10
Mountain View Baptist   10
Oakland Baptist Church Cemetery at Owens   11
Peoples Union Baptist   12
Potomac Baptist   12
Round Hill Baptist   14
St Anthony Catholic Church Cemetery   15
St John's Episcopal   15
St Paul's Episcopal Chapel   17
St Stephen's Baptist   23
Salem Baptist   24
Shiloh Baptist   24

Trinity Methodist 26
Union Bethel Baptist 27

FAMILY CEMETERIES
ADKINS 28
ALEXANDER 28
ARNOLD 28
ASHTON [at ROKEBY] 30
BARNESFIELD [Hooe family] 17
BEDFORD [Fitzhugh family] 19
BERRY PLAIN [Dickerson family] 30
BERRY - TRICKER 31
BILLINGSLEY 31
BRUCE 32
BUMBRY [Bumbrey] 33
BURGESS 33
CAMPBELL [grave site] 33
CARUTHERS 34
CHESTNUT VIEW [Gregan] 34
CLARKE - ROLLINS 34
CLOPTON 35
COBB 35
COLLIER 35
DeSHAZO 36
DISHMAN 36
EAGLES NEST [Grymes family] 37
EDWARDS 37
FARLEY YALE FARM [Thurston] 37
FERRELL [two cemeteries] 38
GOODMAN 38
GREEN [two cemeteries] 39
HARRIS 39
HENDERSON 40
HUDSON 40
INSCOE 41
JACKSON [two Rufus Jackson families] 41
JENKINS 42
JENNINGS 42
JOHNSTON 42
KNOTT HOME 42
LEE [two cemeteries] 43
LEWIS 43

LOMAX   43
LUCAS [two cemeteries]   44
LUNSFORD – WILKERSON   44
MARMION [Lewis family]   45
MARSHALL   46
MASON   46
McDONIEL   46
McKENNEY – BROWN   48
McKENNEY   [also Bible Records]   47,   48
MIFFLETON   49
MILDALE [Goerlitz – Kriegstedt – Wiesklklad]   49
MORGAN [two cemeteries]   50
NAVE   50
NINDE – JETT   51
OAKEN BROW [Low family]   51
OWENS   51
PEED   52
PEYTON [two cemeteries]   52
PITTS   52
POLLOCK   53
PRICE [at Rokeby]   53, 55
PRICE [at Belisle]   53
PRICE – COAKLEY   54
READ [Reed]   54
ROLLINS [three cemeteries] [one also KING – GREEN   55
SHELTON   56
SORRELL   57
SPILMAN – BRUCE   57
SPILMAN SLAVE CEMETERY   57
SPY HILL [Garnett – Taliaferro families]   58
SPY HILL SLAVE CEMETERY   59
STAPLES [four cemeteries]   59, 60
STUART   [two cemeteries]   61
SUTTLE   61
TALIAFERRO   62
TAYLOE   62
TAYLOR   62
THAYER   63
THORNTON   63
WASHINGTON   63
WELCH   63
WEST   64

x

INDEX   65

INDEX OF PLACES   74

MEMORIALS
* * *

DIRECTIONS: In front of the courthouse in King
George on Route 3.

TO OFFICERS AND SOLDIERS OF THE CONFEDERATE ARMY

Memorial to Officers and Soldiers of the Confederate Army from
King George who gave their lives for the South. A tribute   of
gratitude and respect from the Ladies Memorial Association   of
the County.

> 102 names of those who died
> 166 names of those who survived

TO THOSE WHO SERVED IN WORLD WAR

Memorial to those who served in World War from King George.
Erected by Ratcliffe – Owens – Sumner Post 89   American
Legion Virginia during 1935.   Donated by Betty McGuire
Smoot.

[Note: only those names that were starred were copied.]

> JOHNSON, Beanoil
>
> OWENS, Bennie
>
> QUESENBERRY, William O.
>
> RATCLIFFE, Cleland K.
>
> SUMNER, Allen M.
>
> WORRELL, Malcolm

PROPRIETARY CEMETERIES
* * *

HISTORYLAND MEMORIAL PARK

DIRECTIONS: On Route 301 between Route 3 and
Route 205. Infants are buried in
Babyland without charge.

Earliest birthdate: 1855
Earliest burial date: 1926   [re-interred 1969]
Total number of tombstones: 250

OAKLAND CEMETERY

DIRECTIONS: From Route 218 South on Route 603
for 0.8 miles to cemetery on left.

BRENT, Lindora 1844 – 1909

WHITE, Bettie M. d. 2 May 1921 age 86 years

Total number of tombstones: 100   also many unmarked graves.
Note: Rev. C.B. Smith, President;   Frank & Isaiah White, James Griffi,
Ames Walker, and Eugene Brown, Trustees.

PEACE AND LIGHT CEMETERY

DIRECTIONS: Route 301 North to Route 617 East
for 0.1 miles to corner of Route
633. There is an abandoned building which was once the meeting
place of the "Peace and Light Society".
Cemetery is at rear of building.

Earliest birthdate: 1878
Earliest burial date: 1934
Total number of tombstones: 33 with a few unmarked graves.

PRIVATE CEMETERY NEAR FLETCHER'S CHAPEL

DIRECTIONS: Corner of Route 218 and Route 603
               on South side of Fletcher's Chapel.
               Area set aside by chains.

Earliest birthdate: 1873
Earliest burial date: 1939
Total number of tombstones: 15

PRIVATE CEMETERY NEAR FLETCHER'S CHAPEL

DIRECTIONS: Same as above, but nearer road and
               chain link fenced.

CARVER, Annie L. 14 Mar 1862 - 29 Mar 1938 mother, wife of John T.
    John T. 3 Dec 1859 - 19 Oct 1894 husb of Annie L.

Total number of tombstones: 60

SHARP HILL CEMETERY

DIRECTIONS: Route 205 East to Westmoreland County
               Line. Turn Southwest on Route 629 for
               0.1 miles. Cemetery is on right. Note:
               This cemetery is on the county line and
               lies mostly in King George County.

Earliest birthdate: 1871
Earliest burial date: 1901
Total number of tombstones: 36 with many, many unmarked and sunken graves.

CHURCH CEMETERIES
***

ANTIOCH BAPTIST CHURCH CEMETERY

DIRECTIONS: Route 301 just South of Route 205 at
              Edgewood on Southbound lane of divided
              highway.

Earliest birthdate: 1857
Earliest burial date: 1924
Total number of tombstones: 105

EMMANUEL EPISCOPAL CHURCH CEMETERY

DIRECTIONS: On Southbound lane of Route 301 just
              before the James Madison Memorial bridge
              at Port Conway.

DICKINSON, Ada Virginia ... see SMITH

FITZHUGH, Jane Charlotte Washington ... see TURNER

JETT, Carrie Turner 10 July 1848 – 20 Jan 1883 Erected by her husband and
                           mother. Wife of Dr W.N. Jett [2nd]
      Ethel Newton 25 Jan 1867 – 3 Feb 1963 dau of W.N. Jett M.D. and
                           Virginia, his wife; sister of Hallie Mitchell Jett
      Hallie Mitchell 6 June 1863 – 12 June 1955 dau of W.N. Jett M.D. and
                           Virginia, his wife; sister of Ethel Newton Jett
      Virginia Mitchell ... see MITCHELL
      Wm N.[M.D.] 25 May 1825 – 15 Feb 1902 husb of 1] Virginia Mitchell and
                           2] Carrie Turner

McGUIRE, Edward B. [Rev.] 9 Jan 1818 – 29 Mar 1881
      Jane ... see TURNER
MITCHELL, Virginia 4 Aug 1832 – 10 Mar 1873 1st wife of Dr. W.N. Jett

ROBB, Anna Augusta 27 July 1850 – 18 Oct 1880 wife of R.L. Robb, dau of
                           Carolinus and Susan A. Turner

ROSE, Anna d. 14 Sept 1853 in the 50th year of her age "Our Mother" widow
                           of Alexander M. Rose
      William Augustine 20 May 1882 – 12 Dec 1883 son of F. S. and Rose T.
                           Hunter Rose

SMITH, Ada Virginia Dickinson 31 May 1856 – 9 Dec 1953
      Albert Turner 8 Feb 1850 – 22 May 1883 "33 years" husb of Ada V.
      Caroline Alice 1842 – 1908 wife of Henry V. Turner

STROTHER, Georgetta 27 Aug 1842 – 6 Sept 1931
    Kate C. 23 Mar 1844 – 7 June 1936
    Minnie 4 Nov 1848 – 28 Aug 1930

TURNER, Anna Augusta ... see ROBB
    Caroline Alice Smith ... see SMITH
    Carolinus d. 11 Dec 1876 in 64th year of his age, husb of Susan A.
    Carrie ... see JETT
    Elizabeth d. 1759 see Harry Turner, her husband
    Evelyn age 9 years "children of H.V. and C.A. Turner" two footstones
    George [Major] 31 Jan 1821 – 26 July 1916 husb of Jane Charlotte Wash-
               ington Fitzhugh, father
    George 1852 – 15 Jan 1909 father, son of Carolinus, husb of Jane McGuire
    Harry [Major] d. 1751 "Beneath this marble are deposited the remains of
               Major Harry Turner 1751 and Elizabeth, his wife,
               1759, who with credit and esteem possessed and en-
               joyed an ample fortune from which unerring wisdom
               thought fit to snatch them in their bloom together with
               three sons who all died in their infancy."
    Henry Vivion 25 Nov 1843 – 29 Dec 1903 son of Richard H. Turner of
               "Woodlawn", husb of Caroline Alice Smith
    Jane Charlotte Washington Fitzhugh 9 Feb 1845 – 6 Oct 1928 mother, wife
               of Major George Turner
    Jane McGuire 1855 – 25 Dec 1892 wife of George
    Margaret Locke 27 Mar 1880 – 25 Aug 1940 wife of Richard Vivion Turner,
               dau of John and Belle Locke Taylor footstone "MTT"
    Mary Lee 13 Aug 1877 – 19 Aug 1894
    William Smith age 25 years son of Henry V. and Caroline Smith Turner

FIRST BAPTIST CHURCH OF AMBAR

        DIRECTIONS: On Route 218 0.5 miles West of Route 610
                 at Ambar Corners.

Earliest birthdate: 1886
Earliest burial date: 1950
Total number of tombstones: 13

FLETCHER'S CHAPEL UNITED METHODIST CEMETERY

        DIRECTIONS: Corner of Route 218 and Route 603 on
                 North side of Chapel

ACORS, Elizabeth ... see HENDERSON

ACRES, J.T. 6 Sept 1840 – 6 Feb 1923

ALLEN, Elizabeth W. d. 2 Feb 1898 wife of Wm J.
    Robert H. d. 18 Dec 1903 son of Wm J. and Elizabeth W. Allen
    Wm J. d. 24 June 1922 husb of Elizabeth W.

ANDERSON, Anne C. 9 Apr 1845 - 8 Mar 1923 widow of Robert M. Jones

BOWIE, Henrietta C. 1854 - 27 Dec 1893 wife
    Lucy Michial 2 July 1878 - 22 Apr 1894

BRADSHAW, R.B. d. 15 June 1894 74 years

CLIFT, James 7 May 1837 - 19 Oct 1912 Co C 25 Va Mil CSA

CSA SOLDIERS who died in hospital when church was taken over during war. No
                names, no dates, no records of numbers. Space is
                approximately 7' x 30' and marked off by cement block
                even with ground.

ELKINS, Charles Barbour 4 Sept 1861 - 11 Aug 1893 beside Monimia A.
    Monimia Augusta 29 Nov 1858 - 31 Jan 1905 beside Charles B.

GALLAHAN plot contained a weathered stone with date 1880
    M.R. Nov 1887 another weathered stone in Gallahan plot

GRAVATT, Robert 1837 - 1892 same stone as Walter Gravatt and Murnie Pratt
    Walter 1835 - 1878 see above

GRIGSBY, George W. [Capt.] 19 Dec 1830 - 26 Mar 1908 25 Va Mil CSA

HENDERSON, Elizabeth Acors 29 Mar 1860 - 9 May 1936 mother, wife of G. Milton
    G. Milton 20 July 1864 - 20 Sept 1941 father, husb of Elizabeth Acors
    George T. 17 Jan 1838 - 23 Mar 1910 husb of Sarah Jane
    Horace 1855 - 1935 husb of Lizzie
    Infants [6] children of G. Milton and Elizabeth Acors Henderson
    Jas L. 2 Apr 1833 - 10 Mar 1906 husb of Julia A.
    Julia A. 18 Dec 1835 - 31 Aug 1896 wife of Jas L.
    Julia B. 30 May 1878 - 29 Nov 1900 dau of Jas L. and Julia A. Henderson
    Lizzie 1865 - 1900 wife of Horace
    Nancy H. 24 Aug 1852 - 19 Nov 1909 wife of Wm J.
    Sarah Jane 22 Apr 1832 - 12 June 1912 wife of George T.
    Wm H. 1 Mar 1840 - 25 July 1910
    Wm J. 23 Dec 1849 - 1 Mar 1912 husb of Nancy H.

HERNDON, Bernice 8 Aug 1905 - 28 Apr 1906 child of Benjamin T. and Nettie M.
    James B. 26 Feb 1900 - 18 Apr 1900 child of Benjamin T. and Nettie M.
    Meredith T. 15 Apr 1898 - 26 Aug 1908 child of Benjamin T. and Nettie M.
    Oranel 1 Aug 1896 - 25 Oct 1896 child of Benjamin T. and Nettie M.

JENKINS, Thadeus 9 Dec 1832 - 1 May 1895

JONES, Anne C. Anderson ... see ANDERSON
    Ashton 29 Aug 1862 - 5 Apr 1938 husb of Prigie A.
    Gordon 17 Sept 1855 - 13 Jan 1954 father, husb of Lucie M.
    Infant daughter of Gordon and Lucie M.
    Lucie M. 1 Jan 1861 - 25 Dec 1920 wife of Gordon
    Myrtle b & d 23 June 1898 dau of G. and L.M. Jones
    Prigie A. 22 Feb 1860 - 8 June 1902 wife of Ashton

LANGLEY, Charles Co K 30 Va Inf CSA no dates husb of Martha E.
    Martha E. d. 27 May 1918 77 years wife of Charles

OWEN, Wm M. 5 Oct 1855 - 24 Nov 1890

PRATT, Murnie E. 1855 - 1945 same stone as Walter and Robert Gravatt

TRIGGER, C. small flat stone no dates with initials only. Two of these "C.T."
    H. as above
    J. as above

TRIGGER, L. small flat stones without dates, initials only. Two of these "L.T."
    M. as above
    Stanfield 1831 – 1915

WALKER, George W. 5 Nov 1851 – 1 Dec 1929 husb of Mary D. Wallace
    Mary D. Wallace ... see WALLACE

WALLACE, Mary D. 18 May 1846 – 9 Apr 1923 wife of George W. Walker

WILLIAMS, Eliza very weathered stone in Trigger plot

FULL GOSPEL REVIVAL CENTER CEMETERY

DIRECTIONS: 1.5 miles North of Route 3 on Route 610

Earliest birthdate: 1862
Earliest burial date: 1932
Total number of tombstones: 9 plus 4 wooden markers and many unmarked
                       graves.

GOOD HOPE BAPTIST CHURCH CEMETERY AT NINDE

DIRECTIONS: Corner Route 218 and Route 619. Note: Only
                 the following two graves were found.

GAINEY, Zachariah [Rev.] 8 Sept 1850 – 9 Mar 1910 Pastor of Goodhope Baptist
               Church of King George, Virginia and of Grants Hill
               Baptist Church of Westmoreland, Virginia.

WATTS, Robert [Rev.] 1870 – 1930 Late Pastor of Good Hope Church 1910 –1930

GRACE METHODIST CHURCH CEMETERY
Established 1880

DIRECTIONS: Route 3 East to 0.2 miles beyond Westmoreland
               County line. Then right on Route 634 for 0.3
               miles to church and cemetery on right. Note:
               This cemetery is in Westmoreland County, but
               most of the burials have been from Nash and
               Slaw funeral home in King George.

BOWLER, C.S. no dates

BOWLER, Ellen 18_8 – 1888
    Emily no dates
    Minnie no dates
    Wm M. no dates

HAYES, Charles Martin d. 29 June 1869 5 months 6 days son of Josiah and
                          Sarah L. Hayes
    Hettie Mabel d. 25 June 1882 7 months 3 days dau of Josiah and Sarah L.

JONES, Elizabeth L. Payne 1856 – 1937 wife of James Franklin Jones
    J. Frank 25 Aug 1848 – 21 Jan 1919 husb of Elizabeth L. Payne

KING, A. 2 May 1846 – 31 Dec 1880
    Sarah Adeline 18 Dec 1850 – 25 Apr 1920

PAYNE, Elizabeth L. ... see JONES

[ ] LASS, Lota P. ? Mar 1879? mother, wife of F.M. [ ] lass, very weathered stone

Total number of tombstones: 116

HANOVER BAPTIST CHURCH CEMETERY

DIRECTIONS: Route 301 North from Route 3 to Route 611
                   East for 0.2 miles to church and cemetery
                   on right.

CARVER, W.A. 10 Dec 1848 – 1 Dec 1913

COAKLEY, Mary Ellen ... see POTTS

FITZHUGH, Marcellus T. 16 Feb 1847 – 19 Mar 1906 husb of Sarah A. McDaniel
    Sarah A. McDaniel 10 Nov 1847 – 9 July 1933 wife of Marcellus T.

McDANIEL, Sarah A. ... see FITZHUGH

POTTS, Alexander 1850 – 1937 husb of Mary E.
    Mary Ellen Coakley 1852 – 1937 wife of Alexander

PRICE, Benjamin F. 6 May 1842 – 23 Aug 1915 Cpl 30 Va Inf CSA

ROGERS, James E. 11 Aug 1843 – 20 Dec 1915

ROLLINS, Ann L. 1867 – 1900 wife of William B.
    William B. 1865 – 1946 husb of Ann L.

SCOTT, Laura no dates dau of David and Hazel Brownley Scott born in Essex
                       County, Virginia died in King George, Virginia.

WHITE, John B. Trc 9 Va Cav CSA no dates

LAMB'S CREEK CHURCH CEMETERY

DIRECTIONS: Route 3 to Route 694 North for 0.1 miles.
Church and cemetery on right. Note: Lamb's
Creek Church has been in use since 1710. It
was removed from Muddy Creek site and re-
erected in 1769 - 1770. The church yard is
said to be "full of Revolutionary War Soldiers".

ALLEN, A.M. no dates with J.A. Ferrell, L.A. Carver and F. Carver

BUCKLEY, Ida 1883 - 1963

CARVER, F. no dates with J. A. Ferrell, L.A. Carver and A.M. Allen
  J. no dates
  L.A. no dates with J.A. Ferrell, F. Carver and A.M. Allen

FERRELL, Delphia A. d. 28 Dec 1906 78 years mother of Mrs. George W. Sorrell
  J.A. no dates with A.M.Allen, F. Carver and L.A. Carver
  J.H. no dates
  W. no dates

MARSHALL, S.J. May 1865 - 1963

McKENNE, W.H. no dates

NEWTON, Fannie B. 1857 - 1926 wife of James B.
  James B. 1856 - 1923 husb of Fannie B.

LITTLE ARK BAPTIST CHURCH CEMETERY
NEW SECTION

DIRECTIONS: From Route 218 East to Route 624 Northeast at
Owens for 1.6 miles to brick church and cemetery
on left.

Earliest birthdate: 1859
Earliest burial date: 1919
Total number of tombstones: 107 plus some unmarked graves

LITTLE ARK BAPTIST CHURCH CEMETERY
OLD SECTION

DIRECTIONS: As above, but follow narrow older road for 0.4
miles past more modern cemetery above. Note:
old section is overgrown, but is being cleaned.
Many unmarked graves and homecast markers.

TYLER, Arthur L. 1868 – 1886
  Bennie d. 7 Nov 1909
  Eddie d. 5 Apr 1909
  Louis d. 21 May 1905 husb of Sallie
  Sallie d. 23 Sept 1923 wife of Louis

Total number of Tombstones: 37 plus many sunken, unmarked graves.

MONTAGUE BAPTIST CHURCH CEMETERY

   DIRECTIONS: On Route 631 near intersection of Route 610
       just South of Route 3.

CHINAULT, M. J. [Mrs.] 17 July 1840 – 3 June 1936

GARRETT, Mary E. 29 Nov 1823 – 10 Mar 1903 wife of Reuben, mother
  Reuben 8 May 1824 – 24 May 1902 husb of Mary E., father

HARRIS, Herby F. 15 Oct 1885 – 2 July 1893 son

INSCOE, Cordelia 24 Mar 1846 – 16 Feb 1934 similar stone to J.F. Inscoe,
       fenced with J.F. Inscoe and Alice Lee
  J.F. 2 Sept 1844 – 27 Aug 1923 husb of Cordelia, fenced with Cordelia
    and Alice Lee

JENKINS, Malinda 24 Dec 1852 – 2 Jan 1916 wife of Robert P.
  Robert P. 17 Mar 1849 – 6 July 1917

LEE, Alice 14 June 1875 – 22 July 1915 mother, fenced with J.F. and Cordelia
      Inscoe
  Annie T. 20 June 1848 – 21 Sept 1895
  Joseph 26 June 1848 – 30 May 1900 Flag husb of Annie T.

MOUNTAIN VIEW BAPTIST CHURCH CEMETERY

FOUNDED 1895

   DIRECTIONS: On Route 600 1.5 miles North of Route 218.

ALLEN, Jas S. 13 Dec 1849 – 15 Mar 1933
  Wm Sanford 21 Aug 1849 – 17 Mar 1928

BROOKS, Barney d. 21 Apr 1935 age 85 years
  Carrie Clift 15 Mar 1877 – 10 July 1954

CLIFT, Carrie ... see BROOKS
  Marias 17 Sept 1848 – 6 Dec 1921

DODD, Alexander d. 29 May 1916 78 years father
  John 14 Dec 1835 – 4 May 1917

FINNALL, Eliza 15 Aug 1839 - 18 Oct 1913 mother, wife of James
    James 1839 - 1915 father, husb of Eliza

GRIGSBY, Marcess S. 8 Aug 1851 - 24 Jan 1925 husb of Mary L.
    Mary L. 10 Aug 1855 - 1 June 1895 wife of Marcess S.

HENDERSON, Eli M. June 1851 - July 1920 husb of Mary M.
    Elizabeth d. 10 Feb 1898 mother
    Mary A. 29 Oct 1835 - 5 June 1918 mother
    Mary M. 2 Feb 1850 - 25 Mar 1914 wife of Eli M.
    Otis 6 June 1899 - 18 Sept 1899

JONES, Belle 6 June 1856 - 5 Sept 1949 wife of Sidney
    Sidney 13 Jan 1850 - 17 Dec 1927 husb of Belle

MORGAN, James Wm 25 May 1846 - 4 Jan 1925

MURPHY, Wm H. 29 July 1846 - 25 May 1928 father

OAKLAND BAPTIST CHURCH CEMETERY AT OWENS

DIRECTIONS: Corner of Route 206 and Route 218 at Owens.

COAKLEY, Nancy 1802 - 1888

GRIFFIN, Martha ... see ROSE

OWENS, Mary S. 1839 - 1904 wife of Rev. Wm W. Owens
    Wm W. [Rev.] 1834 - 1923 husb of Mary S.

PARKER, John d. 11 Aug 1856 age 60th year

PEED, Jennie 3 Apr 1850 - 20 Aug 1913
    John N. 11 Mar 1843 - 20 Feb 1935 2 Corp G.O. 1 9 Va Cav CSA
    Nancy Powell 22 Dec 1823 - 4 Feb 1886 beside John N.

POWELL, Nancy ... see PEED

REAMY, Alexander 1851 - 1918 husb of Anna S.
    Anna Staples 1869 - 1927 wife of Alexander

ROSE, Martha Griffin 5 Oct 1843 - 21 Oct 1929

STAPLES, Anna ... see REAMY

PEOPLES UNION BAPTIST CHURCH CEMETERY

DIRECTIONS: Route 218 East to Route 609 South. Church
              and cemetery on left just beyond intersection.
              Note: Organized 27 Oct 1929 by W.H.Tyler.
              Church rebuilt in 1963 by Rev W.M. Brown.

Earliest birthdate: 1883
Earliest burial date: 1912
Total number of tombstones: 33

POTOMAC BAPTIST CHURCH CEMETERY

DIRECTIONS: Route 218 East to Route 609 South for 0.7 miles
              to church and cemetery on left. Note: The old
              section of the cemetery is to the South of the
              present church and has concrete steps leading
              up from the road as if to a church. The new
              section is to the North of the church.

BAXTER, Lizzett V. 23 June 1857 – 12 Apr 1884 wife of Wm
        W.H. sr. 1851 – 1929 husb of Lizzett V.

BOWIE, Rebecca F. ... see GRIGSBY

BRUCE, Sallie ... see PURKS

CARPENTER, Edmonia 3 Oct 1898 – 29 Oct 1916 dau of J.H. and N. Carpenter
        John H. 1853 – 1943 husb of Nannie B.
        Nannie B. 1862 – 1942 wife of John H.
        Son 3 Nov 1885 – 15 Nov 1885 same stone as Edmonia, son of J.H. and
                            Nannie B. Carpenter

COAKLEY, Daniel W. 18 Jan 1850 – 29 Oct 1922 husb of Sarah A., same stone as
                            Harry B. and Sarah A.
        Harry B. 8 Nov 1896 – 15 Aug 1942 see above
        Sarah A. 8 May 1856 – 2 Feb 1922 wife of Daniel W.

CONWAY, Katherine ... see GRIGSBY

DeSHAZO, Edward no dates Co K 30 Va Inf CSA next to Laura Ann
        Laura Ann 17 July 1850 – 10 Feb 1943 next to Edward, mother

DILLARD, Ellen Ann 1839 – 1916 mother, wife of James L.
        James Lee 1825 – 1898 father, husb of Ellen Ann

FARMER, Charles Nicholas 24 Dec 1855 – 28 May 1926 husb of Edith W.
        Edith Walker 26 May 1857 – 3 June 1907 wife of Charles N.
        Gertrude H. 16 Apr 1854 – 19 Jan 1916 wife of Wm M.

FARMER, Julia B. 1863 – 1896 wife of Nicholas
        Nicholas 1816 – 1900 husb of Julia B.
        Wm M. 3 Dec 1849 – 23 Apr 1914 husb of Gertrude H.

FERRELL, Mildred ... see SORRELL

FORLOINES, Matilda Lee ... see PURKS

GOODING, Annie V. Grigsby 3 June 1878 – 19 Nov 1923 same stone as William
                E. and Rebecca F. Grigsby "sister"

GRIGSBY, Annie V. ... see GOODING
        Baily L. 1801 – 1885 husb of Katherine Conway
        Katherine Conway 1801 – 1883 wife of Baily L.
        Rebecca F. Bowie 30 Dec 1842 – 24 Aug 1890 mother, wife of William E.
                same stone as Annie V. G. Gooding and William E.
                Grigsby.
        William E. 1 Apr 1844 – 8 Apr 1931 father, husb of Rebecca F. same
                stone with Annie V.G.Gooding and Rebecca F.

HUGHES, Julia A. Smith ... see SMITH

MERRYMAN, Fannie N. 12 Apr 1856 – 13 Oct 1921 wife of J.P. small fenced
                plot with J.P.
        J.P. 12 Dec 1847 – 11 Feb 1919 husb of Fannie N. fenced plot
        "Mother" 25 Nov 1852 – 3 June 1928 erected by her sons Russell G. and
                Eugene W. (just outside the fenced area above)

MIFFLETON, Ella ... see PURKS

MULLEN, John Henry 1857 – 1932 husb of Maria and also with Mary Jane
        Maria 1856 – 1933 with John Henry and Mary Jane
        Mary Jane 1825 – 1909 with Maria and John Henry

NEWTON, Lucy M. 1834 – 1907 wife of Robert
        Robert 1837 – 1916 husb of Lucy M.

PAYNE, Agnes C. 17 Aug 1843 – 25 Jan 1931 beside Patrick H. and Minor M.
        Minor M. 19 May 1894 – Apr 1926   see above
        Patrick H. 1 Nov 1853 – 22 Nov 1941   see above

PURKS, Charles T. 9 Oct 1848 – 23 Jan 1929 husb of Matilda L.F.
        Daniel 1811 – 1881 with Sallie Bruce on same obelisk with Ella, Vannie M.
                Judith, and Ella M.
        Ella 1892 – 1893 dau of C.T. and M.L. Purks see above
        Ella Jane 1877 – 1909 mother, wife of John L.
        Ella Miffleton 1855 – 1881 see Daniel Purks
        John Lee 1874 – 1898 father, husb of Ella Jane
        Judith 1815 – 1900   see Daniel Purks
        Matilda Lee Forloines 7 Feb 1862 – 11 Nov 1930 wife of C.T. Purks
        Sallie Bruce 1829 – 1899 see Daniel Purks
        Vannie May 1899 – 1914 dau of C.T. and M.L. Purks see Daniel Purks

RICE, S.B. [Rev.] 16 June 1801 – 6 Nov 1885

ROGERS, Marie Elois 1848 – 1914 wife of Wm J. same stone as Wm Larence
        William J. 1845 – 1944 husb of Mary Elois same stone as Wm Larence
        William Larence 1881 – 1944 Flag same stone as Marie E. and Wm J.

ROLLINS, Ferdinand 1854 – 1907 husb of Mary
        Mary 1850 – 1917 wife of Ferdinand

SMITH, Julia A. d. 3 Apr 1905 age 73 years wife of Samuel Hughes

SORRELL, George W. 1845 - 1931 Co B 47 Va Reg CSA husb of Mildred F.
        Mildred Ferrell 1852 - 1919 wife of George W.

WALKER, Edith ... see FARMER
        Edwin O. 25 Feb 1828 - 12 Dec 1890 husb of Mary A. beside Edith Walker
                        Farmer and small markers "J.L.W." "S.L.W." and
                        "R.W."
        J.L. see above
        Mary A. 13 Dec 1832 - 9 May 1978 mother, wife of Edwin O. beside Edith
                        Walker Farmer
        R see Edwin O. Walker
        S.L. see Edwin O. Walker

WALLACE, Arthur W. no dates Braxton's Btry Va Lt Arty CSA

ROUND HILL BAPTIST CHURCH CEMETERY

ESTABLISHED 1820   REBUILT 1972

        DIRECTIONS: Route 205 East to first road beyond Westmoreland
                     County Line. Turn Southeast on Route 629 for
                     0.9 miles. Cemetery is on right.

ARMSTRONG, Elizabeth Dishman 1836 - 1892 wife of Henry S. mother of Lena
                        A. Wilkins [information on back of Lena A. Wilkins'
                        stone]
        Henry S. 1816 - 1881 husb of Elizabeth Dishman, father of Lena A. Wilkins
                        [information on back of Lena A. Wilkins' stone]
        Lena ... see WILKINS

BAILEY, Henry 13 Nov 1844 - 14 Sept 1903

CARPENTER, William H. 1888 - 1889

DISHMAN, Elizabeth ... see ARMSTRONG

OLIVE, Clara M. 1895 - 1905 same stone as George A., Thomas W. and Joseph H.
        George A. 1891 - 1910 see above
        Joseph H. 1880 - 1881 see above
        Mary J. 1856 - 1930 wife of Nicholis N.
        Nicholis N. 1847 - 1920 husb of Mary J.
        Thomas W. 1877 - 1877 see Clara M. Olive

SUTTLE, Daisy ... see WILKINS

WILKINS, Bush 24 Nov 1877 - 20 Apr 1955 " D of A " husb of 1] Lena Armstrong,
                        and 2] Daisy Suttle
        Daisy Suttle 14 Apr 1879 - 30 Apr 1951 "D of A" 2nd wife of Bush
                        Wilkins
        Lena Armstrong 1877 - 1920 1st wife of Bush Wilkins, dau of Henry S.
                        Armstrong and his wife Elizabeth Dishman.

ST ANTHONY CATHOLIC CHURCH CEMETERY

DIRECTIONS: In King George corner of Route 610 and Route
678 just South of Route 3

Earliest birthdate: 1869
Earliest burial date: 1931
Total number of tombstones: 35

ST JOHN'S EPISCOPAL CHURCH CEMETERY

DIRECTIONS: On Route 3 in King George just West of Post
Office.   Note: a plaque on the brick fence
says: " This wall erected in 1966 in memory of
Lucy Hooe Boggs and James H. Boggs, Lucile Boggs
Cato, Medora B. Hooe, R.Arthur Hooe M.D."

ASHTON, H.D. [M.D.] 18 Jan 1821 – 16 Jan 1894 father, husb of Martha S.
Martha Stuart 28 Feb 1820 – 2 Mar 1891 wife of Dr. H.D. Ashton

BARBOUR, Philippa d. 11 July 1892

BARNES, Lucy ... see HOOE

BERNARD, Margaret B.M. inf dau of Margaret B.M. and Alfred N. Bernard
age 17 days [buried with her mother]
Margaret Boyd Mason 19 Aug 1831 – 27 July 1856 m. 6 Nov 1855 to
Alfred N. Bernard "To his dear wife, Margaret Boyd
Mason, daughter of W.R. and S.T. Mason, born
August 19, 1831, married November 6, 1855, died
July 27, 1856, and their infant daughter, Margaret
B.M.Bernard, age 17 days who repose together in
the same grave. Her devoted husband Alfred N.
Bernard has erected this memorial of his affection."

BOGGS, Infant d. 22 Dec 1897 dau of Lucy F.G.H. and James Henry Boggs
James Henry 7 Dec 1863 – 19 Oct 1936 husb of Lucy F.G.Hooe
Lucy Fitzhugh Grymes Hooe 9 Aug 1868 – 10 Dec 1931 beloved wife of
James Henry Boggs, mother of inf dau d. 22 Dec 1897

BROWN, Minnie Dickinson 1854 – 1896 wife of Wm W.
William W. 1850 – 1928 husb of Minnie D.

COLLINS, Chas. Read [Col. CSA] 7 Dec 1836 – 7 May 1864 Killed in Battle of
Spotsylvania Courthouse husb of Susan Augusta
Roy M. 22 Mar 1864 – 30 May 1876 son of Col C.R. and S.A. Collins
Susan Augusta ... see MASON

COLTON, Anna H. Saunders 10 July 1814 – 17 Aug 1871 wife of William
Anna Madison d. 18 July 1898 dau of Wm and Anna Saunders Colton
Nina B. 8 Nov 1838 – 12 Sept 1914
William 22 Mar 1802 – 10 Feb 1879 husb of Anna H.

DICKINSON, Minnie ... see BROWN

FREELAND, Elizabeth ... see MASON

HARGEST, Anna Stinger 1854 - 1951 wife of Thomas J.
        Thomas Jefferson 1850 - 1922 husb of Anna S.

HOOE, Isaac Foote 13 Feb 1823 - 16 Feb 1903 husb of Lucy Barnes Hooe
        Lucy Barnes 28 Jan 1839 - 23 Feb 1893 wife of Isaac Foote Hooe
        Lucy Fitzhugh Grymes ... see BOGGS
        Medora Boyd 1875 - 1962 dau of Lucy Barnes and Isaac Foote Hooe,
                same stone as Robert A.Hooe
        Robert Arthur 1880 - 1956 son of Lucy Barnes and Isaac Foote Hooe,
                same stone as Medora Boyd Hooe
        Xarifa Mason d. 14 Mar 1929 dau of Lt. George Mason Hooe USN and
                Elizabeth Grymes Hooe

HUNTER, Frederick G.S. 1837 - 1895 Capt Co K 30 Inf CSA, Judge of County
                Courts of King George and Stafford, husb of Susan
                Rose Turner
        Henry H. 30 May 1850 - 15 Dec 1916
        Susan Rose Turner 3 Oct 1854 - 27 Oct 1912 dau of Carolinus and Susan
                Rose Turner, wife of Frederick G.S. Hunter

KEARNEY, Kate ... see MASON

MASON, Beverly W. 18 Aug 1816 - 21 July 1860 son of Enoch and Lucy W. Mason
                of Stafford County, Virginia. Erected by wife,
                Sidnie A. Mason
        C. [marker size of a headstone, no other inscription, in Mason plot]
        Charles 6 May 1810 - 5 May 1888 son of Enoch and Lucy Wiley Mason of
                Stafford County, Virginia. Husb of Maria J. Randolph
        Charles T. 7 Feb 1893 - 6 Nov 1896 son of John E. and Kate K. Mason
        "E.F.M." [marker size of headstone, no other inscription, in Mason plot.
        E.W. 1844 - 1922
        Ellen 2 Sept 1852 - 13 July 1854 dau of W. R. and S.T. Mason
        Elizabeth Freeland 1844 - 1925 wife of Major J.J.Mason
        Eugine 13 Apr 1847 - 2 July 1847 son of W.R. and S.T. Mason
        Henry Alan 31 July 1851 - 10 Oct 1921
        Jefferson Randolph 12 July 1850 - 29 July 1888 son of Charles and Maria
                J. Mason
        John E. 11 July 1854 - 5 Dec 1910 husb of Kate K.
        Julian J. [Major] 22 Dec 1841 - 24 Feb 1904 son of Wiley Roy and Susan T.
                Mason, husb of Elizabeth F.
        Kate Kearney no dates wife of John E.
        Margaret Boyd ... see BERNARD
        Maria Jefferson 2 Feb 1826 - 12 July 1902 wife of Charles, dau of Jane
                Nicholas and Thomas Jefferson Randolph of Albemarle.
        Octavia 25 Oct 1843 - 17 Nov 1843 dau of W.R. and S.T. Mason
        Susan Augusta 8 Jan 1840 - 18 Mar 1919 wife of Col. Chas Read Collins
        Susan Taylor 10 July 1806 - 7 Feb 1873 wife of Willey Roy Mason, dau of
                Dr. Augustine and Susan Taylor Smith
        W. Cary N. 17 Feb 1858 - 11 Oct 1866
        Wiley Roy d. 27 July 1865 in the 60th year of his age, son of Enoch and
                Lucy Roy Mason of Stafford County, husb of Susan
                Taylor Mason.

MOUNTJOY, Clifford A. 9 Jan 1854 - 21 Jan 1913 same stone as Jemima
        Jemima 29 Sept 1826 - 28 June 1905 same stone as Clifford A.
        Phillis 15 Nov 1717 - 4 Apr 1771 age 54 years wife of Capt William
        William [Capt.] 17 Apr 1711 - 27 Sept 1777 age 66 years husb of
                Phillis. "To the memory of Capt William Mountjoy
                was born the 17 day of April 1711 and died the 27
                of September 1777 his age 66 years. Phillis Mountjoy
                wife of William Mountjoy was born the 15 day of Novem-
                ber 1717 and died the 4 day of April 1771 age 54 years"

MUNSELL, Addison T. 18 Apr 1823 – 25 June 1916 husb of Catherine E.
    Catherine E. 23 June 1829 – Apr 1907 wife of Addison T.

RANDOLPH, Maria Jefferson ... see MASON

ROSE, Catherine Corbin Taliaferro 1833 – 1902

SAUNDERS, Anna H. ... see COLTON

SMITH, Susan Taylor ... see MASON

STINGER, Anna ... see HARGEST

STUART, Martha ... see ASHTON

TAYLOE, George Ogle 19 Oct 1849 – 17 Dec 1904 youngest son of Edward Thorn-
                  ton and Mary Tayloe of Powhatan, King George County,
                  Virginia
    Mary Ogle 27 Mar 1838 – 14 Mar 1914 dau of Edward T. and Mary Tayloe
                  of Powhatan, King George County, Virginia

TURNER, Susan Rose ... see HUNTER

WOLFE, Mary P. 3 Mar 1853 – 1 Mar 1909 wife of P.T.F. Wolfe
    P.T.F. 13 Nov 1850 – 5 May 1909 husb of Mary P.

ST PAUL'S EPISCOPAL CHAPEL CEMETERY

        DIRECTIONS: Corner Route 218 and Route 632 Note: This
                    cemetery also contains two others, BARNESFIELD,
                    which was moved in 1940 by the government when
                    the land was purchased for Dahlgren U.S. Naval
                    Weapons Laboratory; and BEDFORD, which was
                    moved during the summer of 1978. The two family
                    cemeteries appear in their entirety followed by
                    the St Paul's Episcopal Chapel Cemetery.

BARNESFIELD

PLAQUE: "Barnesfield having been acquired by the U.S.Government. The re-
       mains of Dr. and Mrs. Abram Barnes Hooe, This Monument, Sarcoph-
       agus, and these tombstones were removed therefrom and Placed here
       in St Paul's Churchyard, King George County 15 April 1940" "Till
       we all shall meet and each other greet in a fairer home than old Barnes-
       field."

MONUMENT: "On this monument are inscribed the names of all who are known to
       be buried in this yard. The numbers correspond to the stones marking
       each grave. A bracket embraces husband and wife. Children follow
       numerically either both parents or the mother. Six generations rest
       here. Many of the family are buried at New Hope." Monument erected
       2 November 1852 by Dr. A. B. Hooe.

       Since the inscriptions on the monument duplicate, for the most part,
       those on the tombstones, only one side is shown here .

Note: all of this information is duplicated later in the records with whatever else
appeared on the individual stones.

    7. HOOE, Abram Barnes, the Father
   21.   Lucy Fitzhugh, the Mother
   22. blank
   23.   Abram Barnes 3 Aug 1841 – 22 Sept 1849
   24.   Wm Fitz'h 7 June 1842 – 9 June 1842
   25.   Mary Ann 7 Aug 1843 – 18 Aug 1843
   26.   Sarah Barnes 30 Jan 1846 – 5 Feb 1850
   28.   Sarah Barnes 1 Sept 1850 – 30 Aug '51
   29.   Abram Barnes 24 Apr 1852 – 2 Oct 1853 "Our Last"

"ONE FAMILY IN HEAVEN"

ALEXANDER, Ann ... see HOOE
BARNES, Sarah ... see Hooe
BECKWITH, Maria d. 4 Oct 1804 "a relation" #33

FITZHUGH, Louisa Conway ... see HOOE

GRYMES, Lucy Fitzhugh ... see HOOE (two of these)

HARRISON, Mary A. and infant twins 31 Mar 1817 – 27 Dec 1840 dau of A.B.
                and S.H.Hooe (4 & 9) #14 [also a separate small
                illegible broken stone]

HOOE, Abram Barnes sr. 4 Sept 1784 – 16 June 1841 son of Gerard and Sarah
                Hooe. #4. Married 1] 2 Jan 1804 to Lucy
                Fitzhugh Grymes 2] 22 Aug 1809 to Sarah
                Hornwood Johnson and 3] 6 Dec 1827 to Louisa
                Conway Fitzhugh

    Abram Barnes [Dr.] 5 Dec 1805 – 8 Nov 1867 #7 our beloved father,
                husb of Lucy Fitzhugh Grymes
    Abram Barnes 3 Aug 1841 – 22 Sept 1849 son of Abram B. and Lucy F.
                Hooe #23
    Abram Barnes 24 Apr 1852 – 2 Oct 1853 #29 son of A.B. and L.F.Hooe
    Ann Alexander no dates wife of Capt John Hooe
    Arthur Edward 5 Mar 1812 – 20 May 1836 son of A.B. and S.H. (4 & 9)
                #11
    Caroline Johnson b & d 7 July 1820 #16 dau of A.B. and S.H. (4 & 9)
    Charles Thomas 16 June 1822 – 17 Jan 1823 #17 son of A.B. and S.H.
                Hooe (# 4 & 9)
    Frances Fitzhugh b & d 23 May 1829 dau of A.B. & S.H. (4 & 9) #20
    Frances Townsend no dates but married c. 1715 to Col Rice Hooe, dau
                of Robert Townsend. [acc. to Hugh Roy Stuart
                Frances m. 1) Francis Dade, 2) in 1695 Capt John
                Withers, and 3) Col Rice Hooe. She died in
                Nov 1726]

    Gerard 14 Sept 1733 – 29 Sept 1785 #1 son of Capt Jno and Ann Hooe
                m. 11 Jan 1761 to Sarah Barnes
    Gerard Seymour 30 Oct 1818 – 11 Mar 1836 #15 son of A.B. and S.H.
                Hooe (4 & 9) buried at Princeton, N.J.
    Horatio Rinaldo 7 Oct 1810 – 14 Dec 1811 #10 son of A.B. and S.H.
                Hooe (#4 & 9)
    Horatio Rinaldo 20 Jan 1814 – 4 Sept 1837 #12 son of A.B. and S.H.
                Hooe (#4 & 9)
    John (Capt) 1 Sept 1704 – 18 Apr 1766 #2 son of Col Rice and Frances
                Hooe, husb of Ann Alexander Hooe.

HOOE, John (Capt) [a separate stone] "Here lies the Body of Capt John Hooe, son to Col Rice Hooe and Frances, his wife, daughter to Robert & wife _____. He was born on the 4 day of Sept AD 1704 and departed this life on the 18 day of April 1766 in the 62 year of his age."

HOOE, John Thomas 2 Mar 1825 – 14 Sept 1829 #18 son of A.B. and S.H. (4 & 9)
Louisa Conway Fitzhugh 18 Apr 1798 – 31 Dec 1850 married 6 Dec 1827 to Abram Barnes Hooe (3rd wife) dau of Henry and Alice Fitzhugh
Lucy Fitzhugh Grymes 11 Feb 1781 – 30 Jan 1806 #5 married 2 Jan 1804 to Abram Barnes Hooe (1st wife) dau of Capt Benj. and Ann Nicholas Grymes
Lucy Fitzhugh Grymes 29 July 1812 – 21 Apr 1852 born at Mont Chene, dau of George Nicholas and Ann Eilbeck Mason Grymes (she of Gunston, Fairfax); married 29 Mar 1838 to Abram B. Hooe at St Paul's ; d. at Barnesfield, all in King George County, Virginia

Mary A. ... see HARRISON
Mary Ann 9 Oct 1815 – 7 Nov 1816 dau of A.B. and S.H. Hooe (4 & 9) #13
Mary Ann 7 June 1842 – 18 Aug 1843 #25 dau of A.B. and L.F. Hooe; twin to Wm Fitzhugh [Note: this is at variance with information on monument]
Rice (Col) "Col Rice Hooe and Frances, his wife, who was the daughter of Robert Townsend. Col Hooe settled here from Lower Virginia before or about the beginning of the 18th Century and after marriage built in 1715 yonder house now standing and with the farm is called BARNES – FIELD." from monument erected 2 Nov 1852

Sarah Barnes 20 July 1742 – 8 May 1805 #2 wife of Gerard
Sarah Barnes 16 Sept 1804 – 30 Dec 1804 dau of A.B. and L.F. Hooe (4 & 5) #6
Sarah Barnes 30 Jan 1846 – 5 Feb 1850 #26 dau of A.B. and L.F. Hooe
Sarah Barnes 1 Sept 1850 – 30 Aug 1851 #28 dau of A.B. and L.F. Hooe
Sarah Hornwood Johnson 8 July 1789 – 2 Mar 1823 #9 married 22 Aug 1809 to Abram Barnes Hooe sr (2nd wife), dau of Horatio Johnson of Ann Arundel County, Maryland.
Seymour (Mrs.) no dates #30
William Fitzhugh 12 July 1807 – 31 Aug 1833 #8 U.S.N. , son of Abram B. and Lucy F. Hooe
William Fitz'h 7 June 1842 – 9 June 1842 #24 son of A.B. and L.F. Hooe Twin to Mary Ann [Note: again this is at variance with information on monument]

JOHNSON, Sarah Hornwood ... see HOOE

TOWNSEND, Frances ... see HOOE

BEDFORD

BOOTH, Catherine ... see FITZHUGH

FITZHUGH, Catherine Jan 1720/21 – 29 Feb 1748 " Here is interred the Body of Catherine, the wife of Thomas Fitzhugh and the daughter of Thomas and Mary Booth, late of Gloucester County, deceased. She was born in January 1720/21, was married October the 18th 1746 and departed this life on the 29th February 1748 age 27 yrs. As she was a woman of Great Goodness and Virtue She liv'd beloved & dy'd lamented by all who knew her."

FITZHUGH, Francis C. (Dr.) d. 11 Apr 1858 " In memory of Dr. Francis C. Fitzhugh who died 11 April 1858 in Charleston, S.C. age 57. He fulfilled all the duties of life with that fidelity which brought the tear of sorrow to his surviving friends, but who rejoice in the promice (sic) that 'There remaineth a rest for the People of God' Husband of Rosa Spence."

Henry 15 Feb 1686 – 12 Dec 1758 age 72 husb of Susannah "Here lie the bodies of Henry Fitzhugh and Susannah, his wife. He was born the 15th of February 1686 and died the 12 of December 1758 age 72. She was born the 7 of December 1693 and died the 21st of November 1749 age 55."

Henry 11 July 1778 – 10 Aug 1830 d. in 58th year son of Henry and Elizabeth Fitzhugh

Rosa Spence d. March 1849 28 yr. "In Memory of Rosa Spence, wife of Dr. Francis C. Fitzhugh who died at Bedford March 1849 age 28 years. To her husband she was all that mattered and sweetened life, the Tender Mother, daughter, friend, and wife."

Susannah 7 Dec 1693 – 21 Nov 1749 see Henry Fitzhugh, husband

NETHERTON, Elizabeth ... see WALKER

SPENCE, Rosa ... see FITZHUGH

WALKER, Elizabeth d. 26 Aug 1737 age 29 "Here lies the body of Elizabeth, wife of William Walker of Stafford County and daughter of Henry Netherton, gent[n], deceas'd, who departed this life August the 26th 1737 aged 29"

ST PAUL'S

ALEXANDER, Gustavus Brown 1793 – 1860 same stone as Sarah B.S., Judith B.B., and Marie H.
      Judith Ball Blackburn 1799 – 1866 same stone as Gustavus B., Sarah B.S. and Marie H.
      Marie Heber ... see McGUIRE
      Sarah Blair Stuart 1802 – 1833 same stone as Gustavus B., Julia B.B. and Marie H.

ASHTON, Arthur 1835 – 1857 son of Wm A and Betty W.L. buried at Marmion [inscription on back of L.A.Ashton stone]
      Betty Washington Lewis 1816 – 1843 wife of Wm A.G.D.Ashton buried at Marmion [inscription on back of L.A.Ashton stone]
      Ella ... see BERRY
      Fielding Lewis 10 Mar 1840 – 18 May 1911
      Fielding Lewis 1880 – 1923 son of Lewis A and Mary B.H. Ashton

ASHTON, Lewis Alexander 1833 – 1893 husb of Mary Barnes Hooe, father of
                     Fielding L. (1880 – 1923)
     Lucy   ... see BERRY
     Lucy Pratt   ... see NINDE
     Lucy Pratt 1836 – 1842 dau of Betty W.L. and Wm A.G.D.Ashton, buried
                     at Marmion [inscription on back of Lewis A. Ashton
                     stone]
     Mary Barnes Hooe 1848 – 1885 wife of Lewis A. mother of Fielding L.
                     (1880 – 1923)
     Ruth   ... see GOULDMAN
     Wm A.G.D. 1810 – 1840 husb of Betty Washington Lewis buried at Marmion
                     [inscription on back of Lewis Alexander Ashton stone]

BERRY, Ann Grymes 13 Mar 1862 – 5 Oct 1930 born at Mount Stuart, King George
                     County, died at Buena Vista, King George County;
                     wife of Henry Thacker Berry
     Charles Ashton 12 Sept 1831 – 11 Dec 1871 father, husb of Virginia
     Ella A. 1875 – 1877 same stone as Wm P., Ella Ashton, and Thomas M.
     Ella Ashton 1839 – 1897 wife of Wm P. same stone as Wm P., Ella A.,
                     and Thomas M.
     Henry Thacker 23 Sept 1859 – 23 Mar 1939 born at Eden, King George
                     County, died at Buena Vista, King George County;
                     husb of Ann Grymes
     Jane   ... see FITZHUGH
     John of BERRY PLAIN, husb of Lucy Ashton Berry, grandparents buried
                     at Eden [inscription on back of Henry T. Berry stone]
     Laura buried at WINDSOR [inscription on back of R.B.Tennent stone]
     Lucy Ashton of WATERLOO, wife of John, grandparent, buried at EDEN
                     [inscription on back of Henry T. Berry stone]
     Mildred buried at WINDSOR [inscription on back of Roberta B. Tennent
                     stone]
     Rebecca Johnson, daughter buried at EDEN, [inscription on back of Henry
                     T. Berry stone]
     Roberta   ... see TENNENT
     Thomas M. 1873 – 1933 same stone as Wm P., Ella Ashton, and Ella A.
     Virginia 26 Dec 1831 – 23 Jan 1892 mother, wife of Charles A., daughter
                     of Henry T. and Virginia Washington
     Vivian Pratt 1865 – 1943 with Roberta Berry Tennent
     Wm P. 1834 – 1892 husb of Ella Ashton, same stone as Ella A., Thomas
                     and Ella Ashton.

BLACKBURN, Judith Ball   ... see ALEXANDER

BROWN, Nannie Stone 15 Mar 1847 – 12 Feb 1925

CATLETT, Rosalie   ... see WASHINGTON

DADE, Elizabeth P. d. 24 Jan 1932 age 98 years

DRINKARD, Marion W. buried at WINDSOR [inscription on back of W.H.Washing-
                     ton stone]
     Thomas buried at WINDSOR [inscription on back of W.H.Washington stone]

DUFFY, Patrick 22 Mar 1844 – 16 Mar 1906 In memory of a faithful man by the
                     Grymes family

FITZHUGH, Caroline P. Turner, wife of Drury Bolling buried at BEDFORD
                     grandparents [inscription on back of J.B.Fitzhugh]
     Carrie Alice 1858 – 1892 dau of Henry S. and Jane B. Fitzhugh
     Drury Bolling 1813 – 1883 buried at BEDFORD husb of Caroline P. Turner
                     grandparents[inscription on back of J.B. Fitzhugh]
FITZ-HUGH, Francis Conway 1847 – 1918 husb of Lola R.
FITZHUGH, Henry Stith 1836 – 1905 husb of Jane B., father of Carrie A.

FITZHUGH, Jane Berry 1836 - 1874 wife of Henry S., mother of Carrie A.

FITZ-HUGH, Lola Ruggles 1848 - 1926 wife of Francis C.

GOODE, Benjamin husb of Genevieve Gouldman, buried at SHELLFIELD in Westmoreland County, Virginia [inscription on back of
 A.S.Gouldman stone]
 Genevieve Gouldman wife of Benjamin, dau of George J. and Ida S. Gouldman, sister, buried at SHELLFIELD in Westmoreland
 County, Virginia [inscription on back of A.S.Gould-
 man stone]

GOULDMAN, Arthur Stainback 25 Oct 1880 - 23 Sept 1965 brother of Harold M.
 Bessie Taylor wife of Robert H. buried at SHELLFIELD in Westmoreland
 County, Virginia [inscription on back of A.S. Gould-
 man stone]
 Emmett Jesse brother, buried at SHELLFIELD, Westmoreland County,
 Virginia [inscription on back of A.S.Gouldman stone]
 Genevieve ... see GOODE
 George Jesse husb of Ida Stainback buried at SHELLFIELD, Westmoreland
 County, Virginia; father [inscription on back of
 A.S. Gouldman stone]
 Harold Moore 9 Sept 1890 - 29 Apr 1965 husb of Ruth A. bro of Arthur S.
 Ida Stainback mother, wife of George J. buried at SHELLFIELD, West-
 moreland County, Virginia [inscription on back of
 A.S. Gouldman stone]
 Robert Henry husb of Bessie Taylor brother, buried at SHELLFIELD in
 Westmoreland County, Virginia [inscription on back
 of A.S.Gouldman stone]
 Ruth Ashton 8 Oct 1893 - 25 June 1958 wife of Harold M.

GRYMES, Ann ... see BERRY
 Benjamin Richard 15 Aug 1830 - 12 Sept 1913 father, husb of Rebecca J.
 Elizabeth Hansford 5 Jan 1827 - 11 Feb 1919 wife of Georg E., mother
 of Kate
 Georg Edmund 14 Feb 1825 - 19 Nov 1897 husb of Eliz W., father of Kate
 Kate 25 Apr 1866 - 7 Jan 1920 dau of Georg E. and Eliz W. Grymes
 Mary ... see HOOE
 Rebecca Johnson 18 Mar 1838 - 3 Dec 1885 mother, wife of Benjamin R.

HAENECHE, Johanna no dates wife of Rudolph [old stone]
 Rudolph no dates husb of Johanna

HANSFORD, Elizabeth ... see GRYMES

HOOE, Mary Barnes ... see ASHTON
 Mary Grymes no dates wife of Rice Hooe (1878 - 1949) dau of Benjamin
 and Rebecca Grymes
 Rice 1878 - 1949 husb of Mary Grymes, son of Isaac Foote and Lucy
 Barnes Hooe

HOMOISELLE, Caroline ... see WASHINGTON

HOWE, James Phillip 1850 - 1926

JOHNSON, Rebecca ... see GRYMES

LEWIS, Betty Washington ... see ASHTON

McGUIRE, Marie Heber Alexander 1832 - 1882 wife of Rev. Wm McGuire same
 stone as Gustavus, Sarah, and Judith Alexander

NINDE, F. Fairfax (M.D.) 1850 - 1903 husb of Lucy P.
 Genevieve A. 1902 - 1908 between F.Fairfax and Lucy P. Ninde

NINDE, Lucy Pratt Ashton May 1877 - Oct 1943 wife of F. Fairfax Ninde

PRATT, Lucy   ...   see   ASHTON
  Vivian   ...   see   BERRY

RUGGLES, Lola   ...   see   FITZ - HUGH

RUSSELL, Joseph Parker d. 3 June 1853   age 5 days   son of Rev. Joseph A. and
        Sarah E. Russell

STAINBACK, Ida   ...   see   GOULDMAN

STEWART, Edmund Lee d. 1857 age 6 years son of Rev. K.J. and Hannah Lee
        Stewart, brother of James V.D. "Two little
        brothers"
  James Van Dyme d. 1857 age 4 years son of Rev. K.J. and Hannah Lee
        Stewart, brother of Edmund L. "Two little brothers"

STONE, Nannie   ...   see   BROWN

STUART, Sarah Blair   ...   see   ALEXANDER

TAYLOR, Bessie   ...   see   GOULDMAN

TENNENT, Roberta Berry 1862 - 1941   with Vivian Pratt Berry

THORNTON, Cecelia P. Washington 15 Oct 1838 - 22 Dec 1931 age 93 wife of
        Wade A.

TURNER, Caroline P.   ...   see   FITZHUGH

WASHINGTON, Caroline Homoiselle 26 Apr 1849 - 5 Aug 1930
  Cecelia P.   ...   see THORNTON
  Henry T. 19 Jan 1802 - 10 June 1855 born at SPY HILL, King George
        County, Virginia, died at WINDSOR, King George
        County, Virginia father, husb of Virginia
  Lucinda buried at WINDSOR [inscription on back of Wm H Washington stone]
  Marion   ...   see   DRINKARD
  Rosalie Catlett 1850 - 1906 mother, wife of Wm Henry
  Virginia 25 Nov 1812 - 21 Jan 1871 born at EAGLES NEST, King George
        County, Virginia died at WINDSOR, King George
        County, Virginia wife of Henry T.
  Virginia   ...   see   BERRY
  Wm Henry 1842 - 1886 father, husb of Rosalie Catlett

WORRELL, Willie (Miss) 1838 - 1916 "Faithful unto death" in Fitzhugh - Stuart
        plot

ST STEPHEN'S BAPTIST CHURCH CEMETERY

DIRECTIONS: Route 3 East to Route 677 North then North on
Route 609 to church and cemetery approximately
0.2 miles at corner of Route 608 Note: very
overgrown, many unmarked and sunken graves, many
graves marked only with undertakers' markers.

Earliest birthdate: 1856
Earliest burial date: 1905
Total number of stones and undertakers' markers: 67

SALEM BAPTIST CHURCH CEMETERY

DIRECTIONS: Route 301 North from Port Conway to Route 625
East. Church and cemetery on right just beyond
Route 650 on left. Note: many unmarked graves,
some marked with wooden markers, some with hand-
cast concrete markers without inscriptions.

JACKSON, R.R. d. 5 May 1914 age 71 years

MILLER, Henry 8 Feb 1866 - 14 Sept 1899

WILSON, Burnett 6 Apr 1848 - 15 Dec 1897 father, husb of Pauline
Pauline 9 May 1864 - 18 Jan 1917 mother, wife of Burnett

WINSTO[-], Marie Louise 18 Feb 1845 - 26 Mar 1926
_____ weathered stone beside Mary Louise d. 5 May 1914 age 71 years
Note: ?second marker for R.R.Jackson?

Total number of inscribed tombstones: 102

SHILOH BAPTIST CHURCH CEMETERY

DIRECTIONS: Route 3 East for 3.8 miles beyond Route 301.
Church and cemetery on left just beyond Shiloh,
Virginia.

CLARK, Ollie .., see JONES

DAVIS, Bettie ... see WHITE
John G. 5 Feb 1843 - 26 Apr 1927 beside Lucy F.
Lucy F. 23 June 1853 - 12 Oct 1930 beside John G.
M.V. 1867 - 1911 wife of W.H.
Reuben 14 Mar 1885 - 6 Sept 1885
W.H. 1845 - 1910 husb of M.V.

FISHER, Eliz ... see KING

GARBER, Joseph Martin 1861 - 1923 husb of Nancy J., father of Mary E.G.Lee
[inscription on Mary E. Lee stone]
Mary Elizabeth ... see LEE
Nancy Jane Strickler 1860 - 1929 wife of Joseph M, mother of Mary E.G.
Lee [inscription on Mary E. Lee stone]

GRAY, Caroline V. 1822 - 1904 beside Ira F.
Ira Franklin 14 Dec 1865 - 14 Apr 1909 husb of Lucy Q.
Lucy Quesenberry 1857 - 1935 wife of Ira F.

GRIGSBY, William Franklin 29 Apr 1848 - 18 June 1919 between J. Cleveland and
Hunter E. Grigsby

JONES, Julia A. 22 Feb 1827 - 18 Jan 1917 beside Ollie C. and Weston B Jones
Ollie Clark 26 May 1868 - 9 Apr 1928 beside Weston B. sr.
Weston B. sr 25 Aug 1861 - 29 Sept 1944 beside Ollie C. and Julia A.
Jones

KING, Daughter of Wm H and Jeannette Rollins buried at Rollins Fork no dates
    Elizabeth Fisher 1821 – 1892 wife of Thomas S., mother of Mary Ella
                King Lee [inscription on front of Mary Lee stone]
    Ivy Moss ... see LEE
    Jenette A. Rollins 1861 – 1928 wife of Wm H, mother of Ivy Moss King Lee
                buried at Rollins Fork [inscription on front of Ivy
                Lee stone]
    Mary Ella ... see LEE
    Thomas S. 1819 – 1977 husb of Eliz Fisher, father of Mary Ella King Lee
                [inscription on front of Mary Lee stone]
    Wm H. 1854 – 1916 husb of Jennette A Rollins, father of Ivy Moss King Lee
                buried at Rollins Fork, [inscription on front of Ivy
                Lee stone]

LEE, Almira R. 9 Oct 1850 – 31 Mar 1929 wife of Howard
    Eldred 1836 – 1897 husb of Mary A. Rock, father of Ira Franklin Lee
                [Inscription on front of Ira F. Lee stone]
    Howard 22 June 1851 – 12 July 1938 husb of Almira R.
    Ira Franklin 1862 – 1933 son of Eldred Lee (1836 – 1897) and Mary A.
                Rock (1830 – 1910) husb of Mary Ella King
    Ivy Moss King 1893 – 1976 dau of Wm H. King (1854 – 1916) and Jen-
                nette A. Rollins (1861 – 1928) They buried at
                Rollins Fork. 2nd wife of Thomas Eldred Lee sr.
    Mary A. Rock 1830 – 1910 wife of Eldred, mother of Ira Franklin Lee
                [inscription on front of Ira F. Lee stone]
    Mary Elizabeth Garber 1 July 1885 – 23 Oct 1940 dau of Joseph Martin
                Garber (1861 – 1923) and Nancy Jane Strickler
                (1860 – 1929) wife of Thomas Eldred sr. (1st wife)
    Mary Ella King 1851 – 1929 dau of Thomas S. (1819 – 1877) and
                Elizabeth Fisher (1821 – 1892) wife of Ira F. Lee
    Thomas Eldred sr. 4 Oct 1887 – 21 June 1969 son of Ira Franklin Lee
                (1862 – 1933) and Mary Ella King Lee (1851 – 1929)
                husb of 1] Mary Elizabeth Garber and 2] Ivy Moss
                King.

MARSHALL, Rush 27 Nov 1840 – 2 Feb 1916 our father
    Samuel 1830 – 1913 beside Susan J.
    Susan J. 1832 – 1913 beside Samuel

NEWBILL, John Horace [Rev] 20 Sept 1843 – 19 May 1916 husb of Mollie P.
    Mollie Parker 14 Feb 1853 – 20 Jan 1914 wife of Rev. John H.

PARKER, Mollie ... see NEWBILL
    Peyton 4 Mar 1851 – 7 May 1917
    Wm H. 14 Mar 1850 – 28 Nov 1917

QUESENBERRY, Lucy ... see GRAY

ROCK, Mary A. ... see LEE

ROLLINS, Jennette A. ... see KING

ROSE, Mary C. L. d. 17 Mar 1923 age about 82 years

SNYDER, Anna G. 16 Nov 1836 – 19 May 1916
    H.J. 7 July 1832 – 8 Feb 1899

STRICKLER, Nancy Jane ... see GARBER

TAYLOR, Charles H. 1839 – 1917 father, husb of Jane E.
    Jane E. 17 Aug 1852 – 27 May 1927 mother, wife of Charles H.

WHITE, Bettie Davis 2 June 1852 – 24 Jan 1910 wife of Thos L.
    Thos L. 11 Feb 1842 – 20 Jan 1924 husb of Bettie D.

TRINITY METHODIST CHURCH CEMETERY

DIRECTIONS: On Route 3 in King George Courthouse between
Post Office and St John's Episcopal Church.

ARNOLD, Bettie   ...   see   BAKER

ATWELL, Mary Alice   ...   see   SPILLMAN

BAKER, Bettie Arnold 3 Apr 1840 – 15 Nov 1917 beside Wm E.
Wm Edwards sr. 24 Aug 1832 – 27 Dec 1912 beside Bettie A.

BOGGS, Sallie Withers 6 Sept 1834 – 6 June 1916
Thos H. [Rev.] 15 Nov 1833 – 3 Dec 1891 "In loving memory of our
Pastor"

BROWN, Joshan M. 9 June 1825 – 11 Oct 1894 wife of Wm S.
Nannie ... see DOHERTY
Wm S. 7 Dec 1820 – 2 Aug 1898 husb of Joshan M.

DOHERTY, Nannie S. Brown 1 Mar 1858 – 27 Jan 1921 wife of Wm J. Doherty
who is buried in Greenmount Cemetery, Baltimore,
Maryland 1883

HAYES, Charlotte Moyer d. 2 June 1924 86 years 5 months beside Isiah F.
Isiah F. d. 18 April 1923 89 years 5 months beside Charlotte M.

"V.T.H." very old, wooden marker

JONES, Maria C.   ...   see   SPILLMAN

MINOR, Hassetline C. 1850 – 1938 wife of John T. buried with John T. and
Sallie A.
John T. 24 Nov 1837 – 1 Feb 1911 m1] Sallie A. and 2] Hassetline C.
all buried side by side
Sallie A. 24 Feb 1836 – 1 Feb 1901 wife of John T. see above

MORGAN, Nellie no dates
Pemmie no dates with Sanford
Sanford A. no dates with Pemmie

MOYER, Charlotte   ...   see   HAYES

MUSE, Sallie J. 5 Dec 1862 – 19 Mar 1910 beside Wm S.
William S. 6 Dec 1842 – 24 Aug 1898 beside Sallie J.

RATCLIFFE, S.A. 22 June 1837 – 25 Sept 1906
Thomas M. 11 Aug 1829 – 21 Jan 1899

ROGERS, Charles W. 17 Feb 1840 – 20 Mar 1929 father, husb of Margaret E.
Co K 30 Va Inf CSA
Margaret E. 9 June 1845 – 14 May 1927 wife of Charles W.

SPILLMAN, Benjamin J. 10 May 1841 – 8 June 1928 son of Wm L and Maria C.J.
Spillman
Lucy B. 30 Dec 1843 – 21 Dec 1918 dau of Wm L and Maria C.J. Spillman
Maria C. Jones 6 Dec 1817 – 26 Dec 1857 1st wife of Wm L.
Mary Alice Atwell 1839 – 10 Feb 1881 2nd wife of Wm L.
Wm Lansdown 13 Oct 1816 – 9 Dec 1900 m.1] Maria C. Jones. Issue:
Lucy B and Benjamin J. m2] Mary Alice Atwell

TENNENT, Jane S.   16 Apr 1831 – 8 Feb 1896   "Beloved Mother"

WALKER, E.E.   July 1900 – Oct 1900   same stone as Kathleen, Rubie and Sallie E.
        Walker
  Kathleen   Jan 1903 – June 1903   see above
  Rubie   Feb 1904 – July 1904   see above
  Sallie Esther   Dec 1901 – Oct 1902   see above

WITHERS, Sallie   ...   see   BOGGS

UNION BETHEL BAPTIST CHURCH CEMETERY

    DIRECTIONS: Route 301 North to Route 617 East. Church
          and cemetery are at corner of Route 617 and
          Route 633. A large wooded cemetery, somewhat
          overgrown with many unmarked graves, many sunken
          graves, and many graves marked with handcast
          concrete stones without inscriptions. Note:
          the three stones below are the only ones found
          with inscriptions.

BROOKS, Louis J. [Rev.] 17 Apr 1890 – 31 Oct 1956 born in St Mary's County,
          Maryland died in Washington, D.C. "Pastor and
          founder of The Peoples Union Baptist Church of
          Washington, D.C. The Pastor of Union Bethel
          Baptist Church of King George County, Virginia.
          Note: This one grave was fenced, neat, clean,
          and well cared for.

DAVIS, Lloyd departed this life no dates Note: this grave was beside Rev.
          Brooks, but outside the fenced area

SHANKLIN, Anna G. 15 Apr 1934 – 22 June 1947 Note: this grave was found
          well back from the church in the deep woods.

FAMILY CEMETERIES
*** ***

ADKINS FAMILY CEMETERY

DIRECTIONS: On Route 610 North of King George near
intersection of Route 612. Cemetery is
on left near home.

ADKINS, Annie L. 12 Oct 1892 – 16 Oct 1975

Benjamin W. 5 Sept 1860 – 24 Feb 1933

Louisa K. 1868 – 1941 mother

STAPLES, Roy 3 Apr 1922 – 8 Jan 1956

ALEXANDER FAMILY CEMETERY AT SALISBURY

DIRECTIONS: This cemetery was reported in a manuscript
written in 1962 by Hugh Roy Stuart. He
noted that there were five generations
buried here after 1657.

ALEXANDER, Catherine Graham wife of John no dates

John husb of Catherine no dates

GRAHAM, Catherine ... see ALEXANDER

ARNOLD FAMILY CEMETERY

DIRECTIONS: Enter Presidential Lakes from Route 3 through
the Main Gate. Get a map and permission.
Follow main road to third turn on left (Harrison
Drive), then left on second road (Eisenhower) to
first road (Lincoln) left to road just before
circle (Kentucky) to fenced cemetery on corner
of Van Buren Drive. Note: The fence is a high
wooden one with broken gate. Overgrown with ivy
and periwinkle. Originally recorded by Ann. A.

Hennings in March 1966. Revisited October 1978
by Dr. Klein. Note the additional broken stones.

ARNOLD, Frances B. Price   ...   see PRICE
    James, second son of Jas and Sarah A. Arnold d. 20 Sept 1841 in 9th year
of his age. "Express a desire to die and meet his
brother in heaven."
    James, fifth son of Jas and Sarah A. Arnold d. 7 July 1847 age 7 months
and 4 days
    Jane Humphries   ...   see HUMPHRIES
    John d. 12 April 1863 in his 86th year Lieut in War of 1812 "Born poor,
died rich in the grace of God as well as in this world's
goods." husb of Jane Humphries and of Frances B.
Price, son of William [Father of 20 children of whom
the following had offspring, viz: William, Mary, Isaac,
John Humphries, Martha, Jane, James, Sarah Buckner,
Elizabeth Goddess, Jemima, Mary Frances, and Thomas
Thornton. from Ann A. Hennings' records]

    Lucy "Our little Lucy" d. 21 May 1872? age 14 months and 11 days

    Mary Gray 24 Aug 1876 – 23 July 1921 dau of Mary Randolph Brockenbrough
and Thomas Thornton Arnold "Faithful in all things."
    Mary Randolph B.   ...   see BROCKENBROUGH
    Minnie Branche Coghill 10 July 1893 – 28 Dec 1896 youngest child of Thomas
T. and Mary R.B. Arnold
    Sarah Ann d. 22 Dec 1848 in the 41st year of her age in hope of immortal
life wife of James Arnold [stone down in 1978]

    Sarah B.   ...   see MONTGOMERY

    Thomas d. 26 Sept 1840 in 11th year of his age, oldest son of Jas and
Sarah A. Arnold "He died to sin, he died to cure, But
for a moment felt the rod. Neither but the servant,
Jeses sent, To call him to His arms." [stone down in
1978]

    Thomas Thornton [Dr.] 23 Sept 1835 – 25 Apr 1917 "Well done thou good
and faithful servant" husb of Mary Randolph Brocken-
brough.

    William b. AD1727   married to the mother of John Arnold 12 Aug 1781
died January 1813 in his 86th year.

BROCKENBROUGH, Mary Randolph d. 19 July 1893 age 47 years, wife of Thomas
T. Arnold, mother of Lucy Y. and Thomas Randolph,
Mary Gray, Catherine Brockenbrough, Austina Nelson
John, Francis, Charles, and Minnie Branche Coghill

HUMPHRIES, Jane January 1780 – 7 Aug 1819 married 10 June 1800 to John
Arnold. Left a husband, seven children, four sons
and three daughters to lament her loss.

MONTGOMERY, Elizabeth Frances daughter of Robert and Sarah Montgomery who
...[rest unreadable in 1966] [entire stone too weather-
ed to read except for occasional letters by 1978]

    Robert Hall 18 Aug 1815 – 21 Apr 1850 My Beloved Husband, "Why should
we mourn departed friends or shake at death's alarms.
Tis but the voice, that Jeses sends, to call them to
his arms." husb of Sarah B. Arnold.
    Sarah B. Arnold 4 Feb 1821 – 9 Feb 1851 married 8 Dec 1840 to Robert
H. Montgomery, dau of John and Frances B. Arnold

left a daughter, infant son, father, mother, three brothers, three sisters, three half-brothers, one half-sister, and many near relatives to lament her death.

PRICE, Frances B. 25 April 1793 - 10 April 1851 married 27 April 1820 to John Arnold, died leaving husband and six children, three sons and three daughters to lament the loss.

NOTE: This cemetery was at what was once known as WILLOW HILL near King George Court House, King George County, Virginia.

ASHTON CEMETERY AT ROKEBY

DIRECTIONS: Route 301 South from Potomac River Bridge to Route 218 South to brick house on left at the corner of Route 613. Ask owner for directions and permission.

ASHTON, Benjamin 1872 "brother" with Martha and George Ashton

George D. 1827 father, husb of Martha A. [Hugh Roy Stuart in 1962 wrote that Mr George D. Ashton bought Rokeby or at least was living there at the time of his marriage to Miss Martha Brown and that the Post Office was established there in 1850. He also stated that they were the parents of 12 children that lived to adulthood.]

Martha A. 1829

BROWN, Martha A. ... see ASHTON

BERRYPLAIN

DIRECTIONS: Route 3 East to Route 607 South to Dogue. At the Dogue corners take Route 692 South for 0.5 miles to first right. Angle back to house for 0.7 miles. This is a DICKERSON cemetery, but was visited twice and since no one was at home for permission, the cemetery was not recorded. Mr John G. Pollock was the informant for the name.

BERRY - TRICKER CEMETERY

DIRECTIONS: Route 205 East to Route 218 North to first
farm road on left into cemetery. Road is
up a steep incline and does not appear to
be used.

BERRY, Clara T.   ... see TRICKER

    E. 3 Mar 1924 – 21 Mar 1924
    John 17 Jan 1830 – 25 Mar 1923
    Leonard 31 Mar 1888 – 1 Nov 1960
    Leonard 21 Sept 1913 – 8 Feb 1914
    Mary 3 June 1912 – 2 Sept 1912

FRANK, Wm B. 26 Apr 1885 – 24 Apr 1935

HALL, Rosa ... see TRICKER

TRICKER, Baby b & d 22 Dec 1900
    Charlotte 5 Feb 1861 – 24 Dec 1907
    Clara T. Berry 10 Apr 1890 – 2 Mar 1967 "D of A"
    D. C. 28 May 1860 – 8 May 1927
    Daniel F. 8 June 1888 – 18 Jan 1961
    Jesse V. 12 Nov 1894 – 1 Aug 1953 Cpl Co F 53 Inf 6 Div WW I
    Rosa Hall 16 Dec 1880 – 13 Jan 1969
    Russell S. 9 Sept 1916 – 11 Feb 1968
    Sarah 21 Sept 1892 – 9 Mar 1912
    Tabitha age 24 no dates

BILLINGSLEY FAMILY CEMETERY

DIRECTIONS: Route 3 to Route 610 North to Route 612 East
for 0.7 miles to end of road, cemetery is
behind first house at end of the road. Permission
and additional information thanks to Kitty
Billingsley, owner.

ASHBY, Mary ... see WHITE

BILLINGSLEY, Addison Poindexter 1870 – 1957
    Almira V. 20 July 1835 – 26 Apr 1898
    Donnie G. Treakle 30 Jan 1868 – 27 Sept 1911 wife of James A.
    Ella Johnson 15 Aug 1854 – 29 May 1928
    Elizabeth J. 27 Aug 1829 – 15 May 1917
    Gertrude G. 23 Oct 1883 – 1 Aug 1967 mother, beside Joseph A.
    Jane ... see HEFLIN
    Jane Herndon 1860 – 1942
    Jos A. [Rev.] 11 Feb 1817 – 12 Apr 1893
    Joseph A. 8 Sept 1889 – 11 Feb 1948 father, beside Gertrude G.
    Julia E. 1907 – 1965
    Laura Ellen 1865 – 1956
    Laura Jane 1836 – 1927

BILLINGSLEY, Lewis 26 Sept 1857 – 3 Apr 1926 husb of Willantina R. Taylor
    Lula ... see HEFLIN
    Sallie ... see WHITE
    Willantina R. Taylor 6 June 1858 – 11 Mar 1910 wife of Lewis J.
    Wm K. 1891 – 1964

GOULDMAN, Florence B. 3 Sept 1888 –   [living in 1978 at Nursing
    Home] wife of J. Walter
    J. Walter 5 Mar 1884 – 14 July 1973 husb of Florence B.

HEFLIN, Eleanor 19 Oct 1888 – 19 Aug 1976
    Horace Ashton 10 July 1884 – 24 Jan 1922
    James O. 23 Mar 1887 – 18 July 1969
    Jane Billingsley 27 Aug 1852 – 1 Apr 1916 beside William N. Heflin
    Lula Billingsley 23 Feb 1876 – 19 Dec 1877 beside Wm L.
    Robert Ashby 4 Dec 1892 – 4 Mar 1958 Va Sgt Sup Co 318 Inf WW I
    William Lewis 1 Mar 1881 – 4 Dec 1901 beside Lula B.
    William Nelson 23 Apr 1852 – 27 July 1914 father, beside Jane Billingsley

HERNDON, Jane ... see BILLINGSLEY

JOHNSON, Ella ... see BILLINGSLEY

TAYLOR, Willantina R. ... see BILLINGSLEY

TREAKLE, Donnie G. ... see BILLINGSLEY

WHITE, Bernard Ashby son buried elsewhere [on back of Mary Ashby White and
    Sallie Billingsley White stone]
    Mary Ashby 16 Jan 1889 –   [living in 1978 at Nursing Home]
    Roberty Ashby   husb buried elsewhere [on back of Mary Ashby White and
    Sallie Billingsley White stone]
    Sallie Billingsley 9 July 1867 – 17 Feb 1965

BRUCE FAMILY CEMETERY

DIRECTIONS: Route 3 to Route 677 West. Cemetery is on
right behind house at corner of Route 609.

BRUCE, Ira Dana 3 Oct 1881 – 5 Jan 1882 3 months and 2 days the son of
    James R. and Lucy Bruce
    Julia Ann 9 Jan'y 1828 – 28 May 1851 23 years 4 months and 19 days
    wife of William C. Bruce
    William C. 29 Mar 1820 – 13 Sept 1859 39 years 7 months and 16 days
    husband of Sallie L. and of Julia Ann
    William Julia 5 Apr 1851 – 7 June 1851 2 months and 6 days son of
    William C. and Julia A. Bruce

BUMBRY FAMILY CEMETERY

DIRECTIONS: Just off Rt 206/218 near Owens on East end of
Route 663. Permission from sexton of Little
Ark Church

BUMBRY, Galvia W. 1898 – 1951 husb of Mary E. [Mason]
George d. 19 May 1927 age 9 years
Mary E. 1901 – 1957 wife of Galvia W. [Eastern Star]
Richard   d. 23 Jan 1916 age 65
Richard   12 May 1894 – 8 June 1947

HARRIS, Beatrice no dates wife of Melvin
Melvin 1893 – 1969 husb of Beatrice WW I Vet 33° Mason

JOHNSON, Katie B. 8 Sept 1881 – 21 Mar 1977 wife of Willia H.
Willia H. 16 Jan 1877 – 29 Apr 1945

PARR, Dean 15 Jan 1912 – 21 June _____ [not legible]
G. I. 1908 – 19 ____   ____ [not legible]
J.W. 1909 – 1931

PATRICK, Mable Valorie 1950 – 1975 wife, mother

THOMAS, Charles 4 Nov 1884 – 2 June 1935 husb of Martha
Martha 1879 – 1959 wife of Charles

WILLIAMS, Gertrude V. 30 Nov 1903 – 9 Nov 1954 mother

BURGESS FAMILY CEMETERY

DIRECTIONS: On Route 301 at North West corner of Route 1101
near Maryland line

BURGESS, Roland A. 13 Dec 1899 – 10 Aug 1956 husb of Viola S.
Viola S. 18 Nov 1900 – 27 Oct 1961 wife of Roland A.

GARNER, Agnes ... see SHELTON

SHELTON, Agnes Garner 22 Feb 1880 – 13 Mar 1960

CAMPBELL GRAVE SITE

DIRECTIONS: Route 205 East to Route 619 East to Route 218
North. Just after the turn is an old two story
house. Cemetery is in field to right of house
near road. It is fenced and covered with honeysuckle and poison ivy.

CAMPBELL, Pearl d. 21 Mar 1844 "Here is buried 1st Pearl Campbell, wife of
the Reverend Campbell, Minister of Washington Parish.
Died the xx1 of March mdccliv in the thirtysixth year
of her age. She died with our dear child."

CARUTHERS FAMILY CEMETERY

DIRECTIONS: East on Route 3 to Route 205. Cemetery is on
Northeast corner of Route 205 and Route 617.
Permission and directions at house.

CARUTHERS, Azeele Hersey 1882 – 1885 son of Carrie L. Ninde and Veolo
Oglesby Caruthers "thought to have died from eating
green apples"
Carrie L. Ninde 1856 – 1899 wife of Veolo O. mother of Azeele H. and
of Edwin C. and others
Edwin Clark 1899 – 1899 son of Carrie L. Ninde and Veolo O. Caruthers,
died " for lack of nourishment after death of mother"
Veolo Oglesby M.D. 1853 – 1929 [Notes: first doctor in King George. This
house had the first indoor plumbing in King George.
He was the husband of Carrie L. Ninde who was born
across the road at nearby Ninde farm.]

NINDE, Carrie L. ... see CARUTHERS

CHESTNUT VIEW

DIRECTIONS: On Route 610 on large curve in road approximately
0.9 miles North of Route 206. Note: Mrs. Robert
Gregan does NOT want anyone to visit this well
kept private family cemetery. Information was
given by Mrs. Gregan who noted she had had seven
children of whom one son and three daughters are
living. She is a delightful lady with a birthday
on 5 November. She whispered her age so it was
not recorded.

GREGAN, Neices and Nephews of Mrs Gregan , also one son and several daughters
Robert   husb of informant
McDANIEL, Mr. and Mrs. parents of Mrs. Gregan

CLARKE - ROLLINS FAMILY CEMETERY

DIRECTIONS: Located at the intersection of Route 692 and
Route 607 on Route 607 across from Dogue Store.
Cemetery is fenced, clean and contains 7 + graves
with markers. Could not be recorded because no
one was at home and house was well guarded by dogs.

CLOPTON FAMILY CEMETERY

DIRECTIONS: Route 3 East to Route 686 East to Route 653
South for 1.1 miles to house at end of road
for permission and further directions. Note:
There are five wooden markers without inscriptions.

CLOPTON, Alice B. 1904 – 1978
    Elcy no dates
    Ella 1892 – 1969

GREGORY, A.G. 10 Jan 1900 – 14 Oct 1966

KINZER, Ernest T. 8 July 1895 – 28 Nov 1976 Sgt USA WW I
    Grace B. 5 Jan 1895 – 27 Apr 1969
    Nocie   no dates

COBB FAMILY CEMETERY

DIRECTIONS: Route 205 East to Route 218 North to Route 656
East. Cemetery is well behind the Thomas D. Cobb
home and can not be reached easily. No stones.
Informant Mr. Thomas D. Cobb.

COBB, Thomas d. 1969 age 42 brother of informant
    William d. 1957 age 77 father of informant

JOHNSON, Will d. 1958 age 72 uncle of informant

COLLIER FAMILY CEMETERY

DIRECTIONS: Route 3 East to Route 629 North for 0.7 miles
then left on private farm road for short distance.
Cemetery is on left in grove of cedars.

COLLIER, Arthur S. 21 Jan 1905 – 12 May 1964
    Sallie B. 21 Oct 1866 – 8 Aug 1948 between Arthur S. and Thomas M.
    Thomas M. 21 Jan 1905 – 22 May 1965

DE SHAZO FAMILY CEMETERY

DIRECTIONS: On Route 3 just West of Graves Corner (Route 605).

DeSHAZO, Minnie N. 1856 – 1933 mother, beside W. H. De Shazo
    W. H. d. 1 Feb 1912   age 51 years beside Minnie N.

HOWARD, John Lewis 31 Mar 1885 – 9 Nov 1941 beside Kate R.
    Kate R. 19 Oct 1882 – 9 Jan 1977 mother, beside John Lewis

MARSHALL, Wee   1913 – 1914

DISHMAN FAMILY CEMETERY

DIRECTIONS: Route 3 East to Route 205 East to Route 621 South
             for 0.45 miles to cemetery on right. Cemetery
             is fenced in field, but there is a farm road
             leading up to it.

BAKER, Susanna ... see DISHMAN

CLARKE, Julier Augusta 21 Jan 1847 – 14 Mar 1876 beloved wife of Robert G.
                        Clarke

DISHMAN monument includes seven names [listed separately] "and many others"
                        erected in 1961

    Addison T. 23 Sept 1824 – 6 Apr 1895
    Anne Edmonds Jones 1799 – 1845 wife of John Dishman
    Asbury C. d. 1 May 1875 age 26 years

    Jennie ... see POTTS

    John 1793 – 1843 husb of Anne Edmonds Jones
    John T. 22 Sept 1855 – 7 July 1889
    Julia C. 3 Apr 1844 – 25 Aug 1908 wife of James E. Jones

    M. R. 16 Mar 1851 – 21 Mar 1880
    Mary Jane 16 June 1827 – 1 Mar 1904 mother
    Samuel 1756 – 1817 husb of Susanna Baker
    Susanna Baker 1750 – 1813 wife of Samuel Dishman

JONES, Anne Edmonds ... see DISHMAN
    Julia C.D. ... see DISHMAN

POTTS, Hezekiah 19 July 1857 – 26 Nov 1952 beside Jennie Potts
    Jennie Dishman 27 July 1883 – 18 Nov 1940 beside Hezekiah

EAGLES NEST

DIRECTIONS: Route 218 East to Route 642 North to Route 682
where you make an immediate right into Eagles
Nest [well marked]. Cemetery is in front of
house.

ASHTON, Martha Thornton   ... see GRYMES

BURCHE, Wm Chase 12 Dec 1912 - 12 June 1913

GRYMES, Benjamin jr 2 Jan 1756 - 13 Feb 1804 Va Capt Col Wm Grayson's
Contl Line Reg Rev War
Edmonia   ... see TOLSON
Martha Thornton Ashton 5 Mar 1858 - 15 Nov 1922
Robert Carter Nicholas 12 Sept 1856 - 20 Sept 1924
William Fitzhugh d. 3 June 1830 Va 1st Lt 25 Reg Va Mil War of 1812

MARTIN, Ida Tolson 23 Aug 1875 - 7 Mar 1975

TOLSON, Edmonia Grymes 12 Sept 1854 - 29 Apr 1947
Forresta T. 28 June 1895 - 14 July 1928 same stone as Thomas H. Tolson
Francis Annesly 7 June 1846 - 26 Sept 1890
Ida   ... see MARTIN
Thomas H. 12 July 1880 - 16 Mar 1959 same stone as Forresta T.
Thomas H. jr 12 Apr 1916 - 18 Aug 1920 [stone broken]

EDWARDS FAMILY CEMETERY

DIRECTIONS: 0.5 miles South of Shiloh on route 623 which is
0.1 miles off Route 3 via Route 647. Cemetery
is near abandoned Union Church, but is not a
"church" cemetery.

EDWARDS, _____ [large stone, face down] beside Lucie B.
Lloyd B. 13 Apr 1873 - 4 Feb 1968
Lucie B. 7 July 1876 - 22 Feb 1932 beloved sister
Lucy E. 20 Aug 1841 - 7 Apr 1926 mother

QUESENBERRY, Monimia 1866 - 1950

FARLEY YALE FARM

DIRECTIONS: On Route 3 just West of Railroad crossing. Turn
South for 0.5 miles on farm road. There is no
cemetery, but one stone was found during plowing.

THURSTON, Thomas H. d. 25 Aug 1785 in 28th year of his life. Note: This man
was thought to have died on shipboard. Stone was

found in field near the Rappahanock. It was later
vandalized and upper portion removed. It is now
in owner's yard near an old boxwood. The grave
has never been found.

FERRELL FAMILY CEMETERY

DIRECTIONS: Route 3 East to Route 205 East to Route 621 South
for 0.45 miles to cemetery on right. This ceme-
tery is fenced and stands adjacent to the Dishman Family Cemetery.

FERRELL, Ann 6 Nov 1887 – 13 Feb 1900 [stone weathered]
    Elizabeth Gray 1 July 1935 – 9 May 1953
    James Austin sr 21 May 1892 – 26 Oct 1959
    Murney I. 24 May 1896 – 23 Aug 1977 mother

INSCOE, Earnest 1938 – 1961
    Mary d. 1923

FERRELL FAMILY CEMETERY

DIRECTIONS: Route 3 East to Route 205 East to 0.1 miles
West of Route 621 on South side of Route 205.
Road has been "straightened" so that this cemetery is easily missed. Note: In addition to
the stones recorded there exist an adult head
and footstone without inscription and what appears
to be two infant graves.

FERRELL, James A. 6 Nov 1861 – 15 June 1939 husb of Lucy J.
    Lucy J. 10 June 1859 – 8 Nov 1946 wife of James A.

GOODMAN FAMILY CEMETERY

DIRECTIONS: Route 3 East to Route 205 East to Route 218 North
to Route 656 to end of road. Then follow farm
road to frame house on right fork of road. Mr.
Jennings was the informant. Cemetery is on hill
behind Mr Jennings' house. There are no stones,
but some forty years ago a couple named GOODMAN
owned the property and were buried there.

GOODMAN, Mr. see above
    Mrs. see above

GREEN FAMILY CEMETERY

DIRECTIONS: Route 301 North to Dahlgren Wayside, West on
Route 652 but bear left beside the Wayside to
the end of the road. Cemetery is beside the
last house.

GREEN, Annie Pearl 1901 - 1920
    John B. 2 Sept 1864 - 25 Mar 1928
    Wesley L. 1875 - 1934

HARRIS, Isabelle Mason 22 May 1829 - 18 Jan 1915

MASON, Isabelle ... see HARRIS

GREEN FAMILY CEMETERY

DIRECTIONS: Route 3 East to Westmoreland County line. Then
North on Route 683 for 0.2 miles. Where road
makes a sharp right turn, go straight on farm
road for approximately 30 yards to nicely kept
cemetery just inside King George County.

GREEN, James Leven 18 Aug 1888 - 18 June 1965 Va Pvt Co D 149 Inf WW I
    Levven J. 22 Jan 1849 - 11 May 1929 husb of Nannie J.
    Nannie J. 29 Aug 1858 - 28 Oct 1927 wife of Levven J.

HARRIS FAMILY CEMETERY

DIRECTIONS: Route 3 East to first road to North beyond Route
677. Cemetery is East of mobile home, is well
kept and is on property being sold by the
Presidential Lakes community.

HARRIS, Annie King 1866 - ??? no date of death, but she is buried here according
            to resident of mobile home nearby. Wife of Thomas B.
    Clyde B. 1897 - 1943 owner of store on Route 3 which is to the front of
            the cemetery. It is abandoned and may not be there
            as a landmark.
    Thomas Baldwin 1862 - 1940 husb of Annie King

KING, Annie ... see HARRIS

RATCLIFFE, Ethel A. 9 Jan 1913 - 23 July 1915

HENDERSON FAMILY CEMETERY

DIRECTIONS: At brick house on right just at western edge of
Owens on Route 218/206

HENDERSON, Leonard Merrell 21 Jan 1917 – 8 Aug 1944 Va PFC 112 Inf Div WW II
Martha A. L. 14 Nov 1887 – 2 Jan 1970 mother, wife of William M.
Oliver Maxwell 7 Mar 1915 – 4 Feb 1964
Wm Merrell 12 Aug 1891 – 11 Apr 1962 husb of Martha A., father

KNOTT, Lloyd Wm 13 Sept 1912 – 26 July 1958 Md QMC USN

HUDSON FAMILY CEMETERY

DIRECTIONS: Just west of St John's Episcopal Church cemetery
in King George. Note: This may be a section of
St John's, but it is outside the walled area and
appears to be a well kept family cemetery.

BOYKIN, Richard Oscar 4 Mar 1894 – 7 Dec 1968 husb of Sally H.
Sally Hudson 31 Jan 1903 – 11 July 1970 wife of Richard O.

CLIFT, Pearl ... see HUDSON

HUDSON, Blanche A. 1873 – 1970 beside G. R.
Charlie Carlton 1901 – 1960 husb of Pearl C.
Frank Temple sr 31 Mar 1905 – 3 Sept 1963 father
G. R. 19 June 1868 – 23 July 1932 a loving father, beside Blanche A.
Gladys Virginia 6 Sept 1911 – 10 Mar 1920
Mary F. 14 May 1838 – 19 Jan 1903 "dear wife" stone similar to R. H.
Pearl Clift 1903 –   wife of Charlie C.
R. H. 26 Feb 1831 – 7 Dec 1907 father, stone similar to Mary F.
Sally ... see BOYKIN
Vickie ... see MARBLE

MARBLE, Jennifer Lynn b & d 19 Feb 1976 dau of Vickie H.
Vickie Hudson 14 Nov 1955 – 19 Feb 1976 buried with daughter

NEWTON, Harlan W. 19 Feb 1911 – 11 Mar 1965 Storekeeper 1st Cl V_6 USNR

STROTHER, Carolyn b & d 1942 "Our Baby"
George Edwin sr 23 Nov 1868 – 24 Jan 1941 beside M. E.
John Thornton 27 Dec 1894 – 19 Dec 1964 Mason, Va Cpl Btry D 41 Arty Co
WW I
M. E. 26 Oct 1879 – 12 Nov 1914 beside George E.

TATE, George Dewey 8 May 1898 – 18 Apr 1950 Mason

INSCOE FAMILY CEMETERY

DIRECTIONS: On Route 3 East of Route 301 behind house which
              is across from West exit of Route 679 onto Route 3
              Cemetery is chain link fenced, clean and in good
              condition.

AGAR, Jane ... see INSCOE

FOSTER, Lucian M. 3 Nov 1844 – 4 Feb 1908 husb of Nannie I.
    Nannie I. 21 May 1850 – 1 Nov 1922 wife of Lucian M.

INSCOE, _____   [--] Aug [---4] – 4 Apr 188_ broken stone, homecast concrete
    Charles 8 – 10 – 1875 to 6 – 27 – 1937 homecast concrete stone, weathered,
                difficult to read, beside Mollie V.
    H.J. 28 June 1853 – 11 Mar 1903 age 49
    Ida ... see POUNDS
    James M. 27 Aug 1885 – 26 June 1903
    Jane Agar 31 May 1838 – 6 Apr 1897 wife of William H.
    Mollie V. 5 – 28 – 1875 to 6 – 6 – 1934 homecast concrete marker,
                weathered, difficult to read, beside Charles H.
    W. J. 4 Dec 1882 – 24 July 1898 age 15
    William H. 13 Apr 1838 – 3 Nov 1916 Co K 30 Regt Va Inf CSA husb of Jane A.

POUNDS, Bruce 15 Jan 1872 – 4 May 1952 husb of Ida I.
    Ida Inscoe 15 Dec 1868 – 29 May 1936 wife of Bruce

JACKSON FAMILY CEMETERY

DIRECTIONS: Route 3 East to Route 205 East to Route 218 North
              to Route 656 East to home of Mr Jennings, informant,
              who described this cemetery as being "down the
              hill" on his property. It included the family as
              well as the family member listed below.

JACKSON, Rufus no stone, no dates   see note above

RUFUS JACKSON BURIAL PLACE

DIRECTIONS: As above except stop at the COBB home which is
              just before the lane leading to Mr Jennings' home.
              Cobb home is on left. Cemetery is across the
              street in the woods. Informant: Mr Jennings.
              This is a different person from the one above and
              is the only one buried at this site.

JACKSON, Rufus no stone, no dates   see note above

JENKINS FAMILY CEMETERY

DIRECTIONS: Route 3 East to Route 205 to Route 218   North
              to Route 656 to white house on right fork at
              end of road. Owner and informant: Mr Jennings

JENKINS, Horace died c. 1958
     wife of Horace Jenkins also buried here

Note: these people were former owners of this property

JENNINGS FAMILY CEMETERY

DIRECTIONS: Route 3 East to Route 607 South to Dogue Corners
              then 1.4 miles South on Route 692 to drive on
              right. HEPLER FARM. Cemetery is near house at
              end of road. Fenced with low cinderblock wall
              and metal fencing. Name given by lady who lives
              at the house. No visible stones. Later Mr. John
              G. Pollock said this cemetery is where Dangerfield
              LEWIS is buried. He did not recall the dates.

JOHNSTON FAMILY CEMETERY

DIRECTIONS: Across from Shiloh General Store and Post Office at
              southwest corner of Route 623 and Route 645 just
              off Route 3 East.

GREER, Nancy Jane ... see JOHNSTON

JOHNSTON, Nancy Jane Greer 1805 – 12 Sept 1843 "our mother" wife of Philip P.
     Philip Potts 1801 – 1867 "our father" husb of Nancy Greer, [Postmaster
              at Shiloh from 29 Dec 1838 to 9 Dec 1845]

KNOTT HOME FAMILY CEMETERY

DIRECTIONS: Route 3 East to Route 625 then North for 0.2 miles
              to Knott home. Cemetery was not visited because no
              one was at home on the three occasions it was
              attempted.

LEE FAMILY CEMETERY

DIRECTIONS: Route 301 North to Route 625 East.   Left on
first farm road beyond Route 650 North.

FRANK, Allie Bertha 1866 – 1944
   Bernard G. 27 Feb 1888 – 28 Mar 1957
   Jeremiah A. 1857 – 1928 father

LEE, Eldred 11 Mar 1836 – 29 Nov 1897 "Beloved husband"
   Mary A. 4 Mar 1830 – 28 Sept 1910 Mother
   Mary M. 6 Dec 1868 – 5 Sept 1898 dau of E. and M.A. Lee

LEE FAMILY CEMETERY

DIRECTIONS: Route 3 East to Route 681 East then South on
Route 627 to Route 626 West for 0.4 miles to
cemetery on right. Note: This cemetery contains only one large family stone. No individual names, no headstones. Fenced with at
least 6 or 8 graves.

LEWIS FAMILY CEMETERY

DIRECTIONS: Route 3 East to Route 607 South. At Dogue
Corners go South on Route 692 for 2.0 miles
to first house on dirt road before sharp
right turn. Cemetery is in back yard. New
owner is Bert Vander Wert. Note: A second
very large stone is overturned and covered
with a fallen tree. Mr Vander Wert will be
cleaning out the area as soon as he is able.

LEWIS, Henry Byrd 17 July 1826 – 22 Jan 1917

LOMAX FAMILY CEMETERY

DIRECTIONS: Not given, but in the vicinity of Salem
Baptist Church from which burial took place.

McDOWNEY, Mary Emma d. 1 Jan 1979 age 77 wife of Ernest mother of five sons,
   seven daughters, 62 grand and 38 great grand children

LUCAS FAMILY CEMETERY

DIRECTIONS: On Route 218 just North of Route 656. Cemetery
              is on right in wooded area. In addition to those
              noted there are five wooden markers.

BROWN, Allie Weedon 1900 – 1966 husb of Daisy D., father of Raymond
    Daisy D. Lucas 1902 – 1974 mother of Raymond, wife of Allie W.

LUCAS, Clarence d. August 1978 age 65 years
    Daisy D.   ...   see   BROWN
    Harry Stuart 1894 – 1974
    Lilly [Lillie] ... see   PEYTON
    Nancy J. d. 19 July 1978 age 92 years

PEYTON, Arthur L. 1 Jan 1886 – 23 Sept 1966 husb of Lillie Lucas and son of
                        Rose and Benjamin Peyton
    Lilly Lucas 7 Oct 1886 – 29 Oct 1962 wife of Arthur Lee Peyton, daughter of
                        Kate and Phil Lucas

LUCAS FAMILY CEMETERY

DIRECTIONS: Route 3 East to Route 205 East to Route 218 North
              to Route 656 East. Behind the Thomas D. Cobb
              house on the left is a cemetery that is no longer
              accessible even by four wheel drive vehicle. The
              cemetery contains many graves, it is an old one
              and according to Thomas D. Cobb has only native
              stone markers. It was probably a "slave" cemetery.

LUNSFORD - WILKERSON FAMILY CEMETERY

DIRECTIONS: Route 3 East to Route 681 East to Route 627 South
              to Route 626 West for 0.4 miles to cemetery on
              right. Joins LEE FAMILY CEMETERY. Not fenced,
              overgrown with some sunken unmarked graves.

LUNSFORD, Georgiana 1844 – 1937
    Nancy Potts 1819 – 1914
    Robertine T. 1849 – 1921
    William Potts 1817 – 1904

POTTS, Nancy ... see LUNSFORD

WILKERSON, Myrtle L. 1862 – 1906

MARMION

DIRECTIONS: Route 3 East to Route 677 East to Route 609 North
to Route 649 East. MARMION is at end of road.

BROKENBOROUGH, Lucy ... see LEWIS

CUSTIS, Ellen ... see LEWIS

DARLING, Charles Tiernan 11 June 1899 – 20 Apr 1926 beloved brother of Nancy
          Darling Robb, similar stone to Virginia G.
    Virginia Gertrude 5 Sept 1883 – 27 Feb 1913 wife of Charles Tiernan
          Darling, daughter of John S. and Attie M. Dickinson

DICKINSON, Attie Maria 4 Feb 1862 – 16 Mar 1890 wife of John Saunders Dickin-
          son, daughter of Fielding and Mary Imogen Lewis
    Estelle Lewis 29 Nov 1885 – 2 July 1974
    John Saunders 23 Dec 1854 – 2 Aug 1937 husb of Attie Maria
    Mary Imogen 13 Aug 1881 – 7 Mar 1889 child of John S. and Attie M.
          Dickinson
    Osceola G. 17 Dec 1887 – 13 Mar 1891 child of John S. and Attie M. Dick-
          inson.
    Virginia Gertrude ... see DARLING

GREEN, Mary Imogen ... see LEWIS

GRYMES, Helen Virginia "Vickie" 1931 – 1949
    Lucy Lewis 18 Feb 1874 – 18 Nov 1963
    R. Carter N. 6 May 1890 – 4 Aug 1950

LEWIS, Attaway Miller 3 Mar 1829 – 4 June 1915 dau of Dangerfield and Lucy
          Brokenborough Lewis
    Attie Maria ... see DICKINSON
    Catherine d. 29 July 1819 age 28 years wife of Fielding Lewis
    Dangerfield d. 18 Sept 1862 age 78 years died at Marmion
    Edgar V. 19 May 1844 – 20 June 1925 husb of Mary I.
    Ellen Custis 18 Jan 1886 – 23 June 1966
    Estelle ... see DICKINSON
    Estelle ... see POLLOCK
    Fielding 15 Oct 1808 – 15 Oct 1878 husb of Mary Imogen Green
    George Washington 12 Nov 1804 – 6 Apr 1879
    Helen Zola 1 Apr 1870 – 28 May 1953
    Jane B. d. 29 July 1849 age 39 years " Exemplary in all the relations of
          life. She excelled as wife, mother and Christian"
    Katie D. ... see POLLOCK
    Lucy ... see GRYMES
    Lucy B. d. 16 Aug 1856 age 69 years wife of Dangerfield Lewis
    Mary I. 19 Aug 1854 – 12 Oct 1951 wife of Edgar
    Mary Imogen Green 16 June 1831 – 4 June 1913 wife of Fielding Lewis
    Mary Washington 22 Feb 1869 – 9 Nov 1902 dau of Fielding and Mary Imogen
          Lewis
    Mary Willis ... see TAYLOE
    Samuel D. d. 2 July 1849 age 13 years "My Son"

POLLOCK, Estelle Lewis 30 Oct 1848 – 29 Jan 1919 wife of Capt John G. Pollock,
          dau of Fielding and Catherine Lewis
    Infant d. 24 Oct 1821 son of Katie D. Lewis and Matthew B. Pollock

POLLOCK, John Gray 12 Nov 1831 – 13 June 1906 b. at RUMFORD, Stafford,
                                d. at HOBSON, King George, Capt of the Fredericks-
                                burg Arty in war of 1860 – 1865, husb of Estelle Lewis
          Katie D. Lewis d. 24 Oct 1821 age 22 years [buried with her infant son]
                                "Beloved wife and child of Matthew B. Pollock"

POWELL, Fielding L. 29 Mar 1916 – 17 Apr 1916 same stone as Mary I. Lewis

TAYLOE, Mary Willis Lewis 1824 – 1885   wife of John Tayloe V [fifth]

ZOLA, Helen ... see LEWIS

MARSHALL FAMILY CEMETERY

          DIRECTIONS: Northeast corner of Route 3 and Route 301. Ask
                       permission at house. Anna M. Marshall, informant.

LEE, Annie Mildred ... see MARSHALL
        Thomas 13 Sept 1816 – 25 Dec 1897 father of Annie Mildred Lee Marshall

MARSHALL, Anna M. 1894 –   wife of Thomas L. sr
        Annie Mildred Lee 19 Jan 1854 – 2 Feb 1906 wife of Howard Marshall,
                                mother of Howard K. and Thomas L. Marshall sr.
                                daughter of Thomas Lee
        Howard sr. d. 9 Dec 1894 husb of Annie Mildred, father of Howard K.
        Howard Kirk jr 3 May 1889 – 1 Jan 1906 son of Annie Lee and Howard
                                Marshall [Thrown from a bicycle or a horse on
                                Christmas Day and died a week later of internal injuries]
        John Wyatt 26 May 1919 – 1 July 1973 PFC USA WW II son of Thomas L.
                                and Anna M. Marshall. [Died of metastized Cancer]
        Thomas L. sr. 1884 – 1940 husb of Anna M., son of Annie Lee and Howard
                                Harshall sr.

MASON FAMILY CEMETERY

          DIRECTIONS: This cemetery was not located, but according to
                       Hugh Roy Stuart in a 1962 manuscript it is at
                       MOUNT ALTO in King George County. No dates were
                       given.

MASON, Charle Anna husb of Mari(s) Randolph
        Mari(s) Randolph wife of Charles Anna

RANDOLPH, Mari(s) ... see MASON

McDONIEL FAMILY CEMETERY

          DIRECTIONS: Northwest corner of Route 3 and Route 301. Inquire
                       at house.

GREENE, Callie 1851 – 1883 "my dear mother, on her right is her mother, next

is her father, William McDoniel, on her left is her son,
Howard Greene, next is her grandchild, Virginia
Greene."
GREENE, Howard no dates, son of Callie,   father of Virginia
    Virginia no dates, daughter of Howard Greene, grand-daughter of Callie
        Greene, great grand-daughter of William McDoniel

McDANIEL, Lucy ... see PRICE

McDONIEL, Callie ... see GREENE
    D. 13 Jan 1841 - 26 Sept 1916 age 75
    George Culver 19 Jan 1870 - 18 Feb 1911
    Hallie T. 12 Feb 1849 - 25 Dec 1926
    William father of Callie Greene

PRICE, Abner Buckner 25 Aug 1862 - 10 Feb 1927 husb of Lucy McDaniel
    Lucy McDaniel 21 Nov 1880 - 19 Sept 1968 wife of Abner B.

McKENNEY FAMILY BIBLE RECORDS

NOTE: Bible records are in possession of Mrs. Georgie
       McKenney Phillips of SUNNYSIDE in King George
       County, Virginia. These records add to the
       information at the various McKenney related
       cemeteries.

_____, Watch d. 10 AM, 10 July 1938 age 13 years

COAKLEY, Cora ... see McKENNEY

GROSS, Albert Franz 26 May 1856 - 7 Dec 1928 m. 19 Oct 1893 to Lucille
        McKenney [Lucy Virginia]
    Lucy Virginia ... see McKENNEY
LEE, Cora Olinda ... see McKENNEY
McCLANAHAN, Patsy ... see McKENNEY

McKENNEY, Alice B. b. 7 May 1844   married N.F. Payne
    Ann Mariah b. 23 Oct 1823 dau of George C. and Elizabeth Q. McKenney
    Cora Olinda Lee 6 Apr 1866 - Aug 1947
    George B. 27 July 1821 - 5 Apr 1903 married to Patsy McClanahan on
        1 Sept 1852
    George C. 19 Oct 1792-   married 21 Aug 1817 to Elizabeth Quesenberry
    George Crabb 24 Mar 1861 - 19 July 1900
    Henry [Harry] Haskell 9 July 1871 - 24 July 1939
    James Larkin 24 Aug 1856 - 4 Mar 1937
    James S. b. 29 Nov 1829   son of George C. and Elizabeth Q. McKenney
    John Quesenberry b. 1 May 1827 son of George C. and Elizabeth Q. McKenney
    Lillo [Lills] Vondell 7 Apr 1863 - 18 Jan 1941
    Lucy Virginia 5 June 1853 - 28 Aug 1940 married Albert Gross 19 Oct 1893
    Mariah Louisa 31 Dec 1868 - 16 Jan 1953 at 10:35 AM
    Mary   b. March 1828 dau of George C. and Elizabeth Q. McKenney
    Mary Elizabeth 27 July 1858 - 18 Feb 1944
    Mary L. b. 29 Nov 1838 dau of George C. and Elizabeth Q. McKenney
    Patricia McClanahan died 24 Dec 1909 age 76 wife of George B. McKenney
    Sarah E. b. 17 June 1835 dau of George C. and Elizabeth Q. McKenney
    William Andrew 3 Mar 1855 - Jan 1928
    William H. 28 Feb 1820   son of George C. and Elizabeth Q. McKenney
    William Q. b. 27 July 1832 son of George C. and Elizabeth Q. McKenney

PAYNE, Alice B. ... see McKENNEY
   N. F. husb of Alice

QUESENBERRY, Elizabeth ... see McKENNEY

VONDELL, Lillo [Lills] ... see McKENNEY

McKENNEY - BROWN CEMETERY

DIRECTIONS: Cemetery is located at SUNNYSIDE, a farm owned
by Mrs Georgie McKenney Phillips. Route 3
East to Route 205 East to Route 617 North for
0.5 miles. At the sharp East [right] turn
in paved road, go straight on farm road to house
at end of lane. The Bible record above will help
in understanding relationships in this cemetery.

BROWN, Edward D. 1832 - 1915 husb of Lucy D., father of Henry,[original
           owner for this farm]
   Henry d. 21 Sept 1881 age 16, son of Edward D. and Lucy D. Brown
   Lucy D. 1834 - 1911 wife of Edward D. , mother of Henry

McKENNEY, George L. 18 Oct 1900 - 3 Feb 1978 husb of Ida W., father of Georgie
           McKenney Phillips
   Ida W. 20 Sept 1909 -   wife of George L., mother of Georgie Mc,
           and grandmother of George Bruce Phillips
   James C. 29 Jan 1904 - 28 Jan 1970 twin to Madline H.
   Madline H. 29 Jan 1904 - 22 Aug 1973 single, twin to James C. [died from
           heart attack on same morning as George B. Phillips
           died]

PHILLIPS, George Bruce 22 Oct 1953 - 22 Aug 1973 [killed in truck accident
           on same day as great aunt Madline H McKenney] son
           of Georgie McKenney Phillips

QUESENBERRY, Alice B. 1795 - 1888 "sister of Lucy D." [Note: from the dates
           Mrs. Phillips wondered if Alice might not have been
           Lucy's mother, rather than sister."

McKENNEY FAMILY CEMETERY

DIRECTIONS: Route 301 North to Route 617 East. South at first
corner [Union Bethel Church corners] to first
house on left. Cemetery is 0.1 mile back across
field in corner of woods adjacent to field South of
house. It is large and not particularily visible.
There are many slave graves in the same area.
See Bible records for more information. Ida W.
McKenney, informant.

GROSS, Albert Franz 20 May 1866 - 7 Dec 1928 husb of Lucie McKenney
   Catherine 26 July 1894
   Lucie McKenney 5 June 1853 - 28 Aug 1940, wife of Albert F.

McKENNEY, Elizabeth 27 July 1858 – 18 Feb 1941 same stone as Mariah Louise
    George Brown 27 July 1821 – 5 Apr 1903 husb of Patricia M.
    George C. 24 Mar 1861 – 19 July 1900
    Mariah Louise 31 Dec 1868 – 16 Jan 1953 same stone as Elizabeth
    Patricia M. 1833 – 24 Dec 1909 wife of George B.
    William A. 3 Mar 1855 – Jan 1928

MIFFLETON FAMILY CEMETERY

DIRECTIONS: Route 3 East to Route 205 East to Route 218 North
                   Next road on left after passing Route 613 on
                   right. Go 0.4 miles to two storied house on
                   right. Cemetery is directly behind house and is
                   currently owned by the Self family. This
                   cemetery was pointed out by Mrs. Wilbur Rollins
                   Harrell as her maternal ancestral cemetery.

BRUCE, Lucy J. 28 Mar 1853 – 1 Jan 1937
    Robert J. no dates Sergt Co B 47 Va Inf CSA

MIFFLETON, D. W. 1859 – 1916
    Forest O. 12 Sept 1880 – 4 Mar 1900
    Rosalie 1858 – 1934

RAWLETT, C.H. 1812 – 1881 father, husb of Martha
    Martha 1825 – 1874 mother, wife of C.H.

Few unmarked graves

MILDALE CEMETERY

DIRECTIONS: Route 3 East to Route 205 East to Route 620 South
                   for 1.0 miles to sharp turn in road to left.
                   Cemetery is on hill to right. It is in woods
                   and easily missed. There are a few unmarked
                   graves, some marked with wooden crosses, some
                   with native stones and some with handcast concrete
                   stones without inscriptions.

GOERLITZ, Cari 1866 – 1943
    Emelie 1869 – 1926
    Henry d. 5 Oct 1978 age 68 years   husb of Marie

KRIEGSTEDT, A. Fredric 1868 – 1941
    August   no dates   grandfather
    August   15 Sept _____ – 10 Oct 1913   very weathered
    August H. 1910 – 1971
    Joseph 1897 – 1924
    Oscar no dates
    Pauline M. 1874 – 1955

WIESKLKLAD, Alma   d. 1933
    Franz   no dates

MORGAN FAMILY CEMETERY

DIRECTIONS: On Route 301 between Route 3 and Route 205 in
              the Northeast corner of Historyland Memorial
              Park.

HALL, Sarah Frances 10 Sept 1877 - 8 July 1967 sister

MORGAN, Fenton 1842 - 1912 wife of J.H. "erected by Sarah"
    J. H. 1828 - 1902 husb of Fenton "erected by Sarah"
    L. V. 9 Feb 1889 - 2 Nov 1915 "In memory by brothers"
    Lorena 31 Dec 1894 - 28 Apr 1978 wife of Rudolphus
    Robert Lawson 2 2 Nov 1873 - 6 Mar 1950
    Rudolphus 17 Sept 1883 - 9 Oct 1970 husb of Lorena

MORGAN FAMILY CEMETERY

DIRECTIONS: Route 3 East to Route 610 North for 1.3 miles
              to small private fenced cemetery on left. There
              are two large concrete markers and one wooden
              marker without inscriptions also.

MORGAN, Esther Darleen b & d 13 May 1947
    George F. 12 Sept 1908 - 24 Mar 1944
    Glenn Edward 30 Oct 1942 - 17 July 1965
    Nannie B. 20 Feb 1873 - 23 Jan 1957 wife of Winfield F.
    Winfield F. 8 Aug 1866 - 18 June 1946 husb of Nannie B.

NAVE FAMILY CEMETERY

DIRECTIONS: On Route 3 West of Route 605 for 1.3 miles,
              beside the Agricultural Stabilization and Con-
              servation Service County Office Building.

MATHESON, Addie Elizabeth Nave 17 Jan 1914 - 10 Nov 1952 mother

NAVE, Addie Elizabeth ... see MATHESON
    Beulah D. 1 Jan 1884 - 14 Jan 1964
    Grace M. 1915 - 1953 Mother of Omey
    Henry Thomas 13 Feb 1904 - 13 Apr 1909
    Homer 7 Aug 1902 = 18 Mar 1978 husband
    Omey b & d 1953 dau of Grace M.
    Richard Roderick 7 Feb 1908 - 9 Aug 1969
    Roderick Samuel B. 30 June 1875 - 5 Oct 1960 husb of Tabitha Maude
    Tabitha Maude 15 Apr 1877 -13 Dec 1941 wife of Roderick S.B. pictures
    Theodore R. 12 Jan 1901 - 24 Feb 1978

NINDE - JETT FAMILY CEMETERY

DIRECTIONS: Route 3 East to Route 205 East to Route 617.
House and cemetery are directly across from
Route 617 and from Nick's Sporting Goods Store.
Owner is Frye. Visited on three occasions, but
unable to record because of bad dogs. Informants
were former owners, Frank and Virginia Austin.
Cemetery is visible, fenced, but overgrown and
may contain as many as twelve graves.

OAKEN BROW

DIRECTIONS: Route 301 North to Route 625 East to Route 650.
Turn South on road that appears to be an ex-
tension of Route 650. Private road. Owner:
J.R.Low

"Our Charlie" no dates

HAWKINS, Maude ... see LOW

LEWIS, Alice A. Tayloe ... see TAYLOE

LOW, Joseph Hooker [M.D.] 28 Jan 1867 – 2 Nov 1929 beside Maude H.
    Maude Hawkins 4 Sept 1879 – 4 Sept 1954 beside Joseph H.

TAYLOE, Alice A. 5 Apr 1837 – 12 Feb 1862 wife of Dr. T. M. Lewis
    Charles 15 Feb 1810 – 11 Nov 1847

WARING, Rosalie V. 10 Dec 1833 – 18 Feb 1872 wife of W. L. Waring
    Thomas R. 10 Jan 1833 – 12 Dec 1880 born in Essex County, died at Oaken
    Brow

OWENS FAMILY CEMETERY

DIRECTIONS: Route 3 East to Route 205 East to Route 619
to Nash and Slaw Funeral Home on left. Cemetery
is behind building, however, it has not shown
any evidence of being a cemetery in the past 15
years. No stones, no depressions, etc. May have
been bulldozed before Nash and Slaw occupied the
property. Informant: Paul Slaw.

PEED FAMILY CEMETERY

DIRECTIONS: This cemetery in 1962 was at "North Hill Windsor"
later called "High Hill" records were included
in the manuscript by Hugh Roy Stuart

COAKLEY, Ginny ... see PEED

PEED, Ginny Coakley wife of John N. no dates
John N. d. at age 93 no dates husb of Ginny Coakley

PEYTON FAMILY CEMETERY

DIRECTIONS: Route 3 East to Route 205 East to Route 619, cross
Route 218 and continue East on Route 619 for an
additional 0.8 miles to Farrington Farm. Ask at
house for permission and for a guide. Cemetery
is in deep woods, across a run. It may contain
as many as 50 graves. It is visited on Memorial
Day by the family. Only one carved wooden marker
was found:

PEYTON, J. F. d. 13 Dec 1925

PEYTON FAMILY CEMETERY

DIRECTIONS: Route 3 East to Route 205 East to Route 684 East
(old part of Route 205). Cemetery is on right
immediately after entering Route 684. There are
10 - 15 other graves, several with grave covers,
but all without markers or inscriptions.

PEYTON, Carrie E. 1906 - 1973 mother, wife of Randolph
Randolph 1897 - 1974 father, husb of Carrie E.

PITTS FAMILY CEMETERY

DIRECTIONS: Route 301 North to Route 614 West to Route 635 North
for 1.4 miles North on Route 624. Cemetery on right.

BARTLETT, Lydia Jane 18 Sept 1912 - 27 Feb 1978

PITTS, Bessie M. 20 Oct 1886 - 10 May 1962 mother, wife of Lewis

PITTS, Lewis 10 Dec 1871 - 20 Mar 1936 father, husb of Bessie M.
   Raymond 1903 - 1924
   Thomas C. 3 Sept 1910 - 2 June 1973

POLLOCK FAMILY CEMETERY

DIRECTIONS: This cemetery was until recently on the old
Smith farm on Route 607 near Route 660. It
was moved to Emmanuel Episcopal Church Cemetery,
but Mr. John G. Pollock who has been most helpful,
asked that it be included as a family cemetery.

POLLOCK, John Gray 20 Aug 1874 - 12 Aug 1959 husb of Minnie Gertrude Smith
   Minnie Gertrude Smith ... see SMITH

SMITH, Minnie Gertrude 17 Oct 1878 - 3 Nov 1968 wife of John Gray Pollock

PRICE CEMETERY AT ROKEBY

DIRECTIONS: Route 301 South from Potomac River Bridge to last
road on left before Route 613. Inquire from owner
at house on right near end of road. This cemetery
was not visited and is not known to the owner of
what is now known as "Rokeby". Mr Stuart in his
1962 manuscript stated: "The Northern portion of
Rokeby was bought from the estate by Captain Martin
Luther Price who married the eldest daughter, Lucy,
of Mr and Mrs George D. Ashton......Mr and Mrs M.
L. Price died and are buried at this old home that
never bore a name that I ever heard of save part of
Rokeby".

NOTE: Their graves were not found with the Ashton graves at Rokeby so it
may be inferred that the cemetery for this family
was not found.

ASHTON, Lucy ... see PRICE

PRICE, Lucy Ashton no dates, wife of Capt Martin L., dau of George A. Ashton
   Martin Luther no dates, husb of Lucy Ashton, Capt Co K 30th Va Reg CSA

PRICE FAMILY CEMETERY AT BELISLE

DIRECTIONS: In woods near the Miffleton cemetery. Informants:
Mrs Ida W. McKenney and Mrs Georgie McKenney
Phillips. See McKenney Bible Records. Not visited.

EMERSON, Mary ... see PRICE

McKENNEY, Alice no dates, dau of Mary Frances Price and George McKenney
   George husb of Mary Frances Price, father of Alice, no dates

54   TOMBSTONE INSCRIPTIONS OF KING GEORGE COUNTY, VIRGINIA

McKENNEY, Grandma (of Mrs. Phillips) who was Fannie Price, dau of Dr Price
                    and Mary
    James Larkin   no dates
    Mary Frances Price, wife of George, mother of Alice no dates

PRICE, Mary Emerson dates unknown, 1st wife of Dr Wm B.K. Price who married
                    2nd her sister Belle Emerson. Note: Dr Price is buried
                    in Texas. Burial place of Belle is not known by inform-
                    ants. Mary was the mother of twelve children.

PRICE - COAKLEY FAMILY CEMETERY

DIRECTIONS: Route 3 East to Route 205 East to Ninde Post Office
             Ask permission from Postmistress. Turn right on
             next road, Route 620. Go 0.05 miles and park.
             Road leading up to cemetery is on left, has a
             chain across it. Walk approximately 0.1 miles
             mostly uphill to cemetery at end of lane.

COAKLEY, Julia Potts 1863 - 1954 wife of Richard P.
    Mary Piper 20 Mar 1830 - 3 Apr 1903 "Our Mother"
    Richard Powell 1859 - 1935 husb of Julia Potts
    William Bevan 3 April 1897 - 3 Nov 1954

HOOSER, Flora M. 18 Feb 1873 - 26 May 1965

PIPER, Mary ... see COAKLEY

POTTS, Fannie B. 8 Apr 1859 - 10 July 1949
    Julia ... see COAKLEY

PRICE, Bettie B. 16 Dec 1848 - 27 Feb 1912 wife of George W.
    George W. 23 Nov 1843 - 26 Mar 1917 husb of Bettie B.
    Walter 1902 - 1909

READ - REED FAMILY CEMETERY

DIRECTIONS: Route 3 East to Route 629 North for 0.7 miles.
             Follow farm road to left to end of road. Cemetery
             is in deep woods and can only be reached by four
             wheel drive vehicle. Mrs. Collier Rose informant.

READ [REED] John d. c. 1966 in Washington, D.C. and was brought back for
             burial with his family. There are many other graves
             all are unmarked

ROLLINS FAMILY CEMETERY

DIRECTIONS: Route 3 East to East end of Route 679 South. Bear
             right as you pass several new houses and through
             one gate. Continue for 0.5 miles to older house.
             Cemetery is on left.

_____, "Patsy" no dates

ROLLINS, Albert B. 16 Nov 1847 - 1920 husb of Sidney A.
     Sidney A. Rose ... see ROSE

ROSE, Sidney A. 10 Sept 1845 - 2 Nov 1925   wife of Albert B. Rollins

VAN NESS, Francis d. 26 Sept 1882 age 22, a native of Chatham, N.Y.

ROLLINS FAMILY CEMETERY

DIRECTIONS: Route 218 West from Route 619 and Route 205. Turn
             East on Route 613 to top of hill. Small cemetery
             without stones, marked by eight square concrete
             blocks. Mrs Harrell, widow of Joseph Wilbur
             Rollins lives across road and was informant.

DICKENS, Ginny ... see PRICE

PRICE, Ginny Dickens Rollins d. April 1939 married 1] Winford Rollins and 2]
                    Algee Price. She was the mother of ten Rollins children.

ROLLINS, Annie Belle d. c. 1929 age 20 dau of Winford and Ginny Dickens Rollins,
                    sister of Joseph Wilbur, William, Kirk, and seven others.
     Ginny ... see PRICE
     Joseph Wilbur 19 Jan 1915 - 19 Jan 1950 son of Winford and Ginny Dickens
                    Rollins
     Kirk [son of Winford and Ginny Dickens Rollins is buried at Round Hill]
     William d. age 2 months from Whooping Cough
     Winford d. around 1928 husb of Ginny Dickens Rollins [later Price], father
                    of Joseph Wilbur Rollins, Annie Bell Rollins, Kirk,
                    and of seven other children [living in 1978]

ROLLINS - KING - GREEN CEMETERY
AT ROLLINS FORK

DIRECTIONS: Route 3 East to Route 681 to Route 627 South. First
             drive on right leads to a mobile home. Cemetery is
             on side of drive.

FISHER, Eliza ... see KING

GREEN, Bettie ... see ROLLINS
    Daphnie no dates infant
    Delda no dates infant
    Erasmus 1859 – 1923 husb of Mary A.
    Mary A. 1856 – 1923 wife of Erasmus

KING, A. Dorsey Rollins 1866 – 1907 mother, wife of James B.
    Annie Wave 1899 – 1904
    D. Guy 20 July 1888 – 20 Jan 1950 husb of Mary S.
    E. F. [small stone labeled only "E.F.K."
    Eliza Bet 1892 – 1893
    Eliza Fisher 5 Jan 1821 – 5 Apr 1892 wife of Thomas King buried at
               KENLOCK FARM, Essex County, Virginia
    James Bagby 1858 – 1933 father husb of A. Dorsey Rollins
    Jennette A. 9 Jan 1861 – 21 June 1928 wife of Wm H.
    Mary Syndor 7 Feb 1896 – 25 Dec 1958 wife of D. Guy
    Vivian 1890 – 1891
    William Ellsworth 18 Jan 1920 – 20 Jan 1950 Va GM$_3$USNR WW II
    William H. 15 Jan 1854 – 5 Nov 1916 husb of Jennette A.
    Zoe 1891 – 1891

ROLLINS, A. Dorsey ... see KING
    Bettie Green no dates same stone as Lovell B.
    Lovell B. no dates same stone as Bettie Green

SYNDOR, Mary ... see KING

WAVE, Annie ... see KING

WEEDON, Bettie L. 10 Feb 1856 – 24 June 1924 wife of W.A.
    W.A. 6 Jan 1846 – 18 Mar 1927 husb of Bettie L.

SHELTON FAMILY CEMETERY

        DIRECTIONS: Cemetery moved to Fletcher' Chapel, but is recorded
        here in its entirity.

SHELTON, [seven stones too weathered to read]
    Esther B. 6 Feb 1900 – 9 Apr 1900
    Gordon W. d. 25 Sept 1917 60 years husb of Margaret D. L.
    John Fred 15 Sept 1876 – 11 Nov 1929 father
    J. [John] S. 1851 – 1923 husb of Sarah A.
    Lena B. 22 Apr 1902 – 20 July 1902
    Lenor D. 21 Sept 1883 – 21 Oct 1884
    Luke M. 1879 – 1964 husb of Virginia B., father
    Margaret D. L. d. 22 May 1943 aged 79 years wife of Gordon W.
    Matt L. 19 Feb 1889 – 18 July 1889
    Sarah A. 1872 – 1913 wife of J.S.
    Virginia B. 1877 – 1949 wife of Luke M., mother

SORRELL FAMILY CEMETERY

DIRECTIONS: Route 3 East to Route 677 East then North on
               Route 609 to Route 648 West to junction with
               Route 700. On Northeast corner is a small fenced
               cemetery. Very overgrown, only one stone visible.
               Other information from a neighbor who did not
               wish to give her name.

SORRELL, Brother of Ms. Lizzie
    C.H. [headstone and footstone, but with no dates] brother of Lizzie
    Father of Ms. Lizzie
    Lizzie no stone, no dates
    Mother of Ms. Lizzie

SPILMAN - BRUCE FAMILY CEMETERY

DIRECTIONS: Route 3 East to Route 205 East to Route 218 West
               to Route 1111. Turn left at second of two drives
               that are almost adjoining. Cemetery is on hill
               behind the Branham home. Fenced, being cleaned.
               Note: This property was originally owned by a
               Mr. George Bruce who was a blacksmith. Later it
               was purchased by William [Billy] Spilman and then
               was given to Billy's daughter Pearl who married a
               Jesse Dudley. The old home is no longer there. In
               addition to the stones that were recorded there are
               more than ten sunken unmarked graves., two graves
               with bases for stones, but no headstones or inscrip-
               tions.

BRUCE, _____[large, heavy stone face down. The name BRUCE is on both
               the base and the back of the portion that is down]

SPILMAN, _____ [base only, stone is missing or covered with debris.]
    Mary L. 10 Mar 1867 - 24 May 1925

SPILMAN SLAVE CEMETERY

DIRECTIONS: Route 3 East to Route 205 East to Route 218 West
               to Route 1111 West. This cemetery is in woods
               perhaps 0.2 miles from the Spilman - Bruce
               Cemetery, above. It contains many sunken graves,
               some with flat rocks to mark their location.
               It was not visited. Informant: Seab Branham.

SPY HILL CEMETERY
[GARNETT - TALIAFERRO FAMILY CEMETERY]

DIRECTIONS: Route 3 East to Route 205 East to Route 619 East.
Cross Route 218 and bear left at fork. Farm is
well marked. Drive carefully and ask for both
permission and directions.

BABER, Thomas B. 21 Sept 1827 - 31 Oct 1872 brother
    Thomas B. B. 20 Sept 1795 - 30 Apr 1871 father

BEALE, Genevieve Garnett d. 9 Aug 1875 age 8 months 21 days dau of Richard
    Channing and Emma Baber Beale

BRITTON, Florence Garnett 27 Aug 1886 - 15 June 1928

BROWN, Belle ... see GARNETT

GARNETT, Algernon S. [M.D.] 2 Aug 1885 - 30 Oct 1955 husb of Josephine
    Belle ... see TALIAFERRO
    Belle Brown 29 Oct 1854 - 8 Dec 1936 wife of Henry
    Emma ... see MILLS
    Emma L. 18 Mar 1825 - 2 Aug 1906 wife of Thomas S.
    Florence ... see BRITTON
    Henry T. 1861 - 1933 husb of Belle B.
    John 2 Oct 1861 - 21 Aug 1911
    Josephine 6 Feb 1874 - 28 Dec 1958 wife of A.S. Garnett
    Josephine Ijams 1 Nov 1882 - 6 Dec 1968 dau of Henry and Belle Garnett
    Laura Hayward 20 Jan 1888 - 20 Jan 1970 wife of Thomas S.
    Miyoko 1928 - 1971 wife of Thomas Stuart jr "Sandy"
    Stuart Bankhead 1 May 1860 - 9 Dec 1882 son of Thos S. and E. L. Garnett,
        grandson of Thos B. B. Baber
    Thomas Baber 4 May 1853 - 9 Apr 1926 son of Thomas S. and Emma L.
        Garnett
    Thomas S. 19 Apr 1825 - 4 May 1863 husb of Emma L., Col 49th Va Vol CSA
        Killed at Chancellorville, Virginia
    Thomas Stuart 17 Mar 1881 - 9 Feb 1961 husb of Laura H.
    Thomas Stuart jr. 1915 - 1974 husb of Miyoko "Sandy"
    William B. 1884 - 1934

HAYWARD, Laura ... see GARNETT

MILLS, Emma Garnett 1849 - 1936

TALIAFERRO, Belle Garnett 28 June 1917 -   wife of Edwin Maywood
    Taliaferro
    Edwin Maywood 28 Sept 1911 - 27 Jan 1967 husb of Belle G.

SPY HILL SLAVE CEMETERY

DIRECTIONS: Route 3 East to Route 205 East to Route 619 East.
Cross Route 218 and bear right at Spy Hill farm
road turn for 0.2 miles. Watch for ivy growing
over embankment on right side of road. Cemetery
occupies approximately 2½ acres. There are as
many as 100 graves marked with concrete and wooden
markers without inscriptions. There are many more
that are sunken and unmarked. This cemetery is
thought to date back to the 1700's and early 1800's
Only the one stone listed below was legible.

PAYTON, Harvey Oct 1910 – 18 Apr 1948

STAPLES FAMILY CEMETERY

DIRECTIONS: Route 3 East to Route 206 East to the Northeast
corner of Route 610. The cemetery is hidden by
honeysuckle, is fenced and very neat once you
enter gate.

STAPLES, Alvin J. d. 11 Dec 1976 age 76 years
    Baby girl b & d 2 Feb 1962
    Eva Etta 15 Aug 1883 – 21 June 1950 mother
    Francis C. 21 Oct 1921 – 25 Feb 1940 son
    Milton Turner sr. d. 26 Feb 1971 age 70 years
    Norman S. 1 Jan 1916 – 26 Jan 1919

STAPLES FAMILY CEMETERY

DIRECTIONS: Route 3 East to Route 607 East. Pass Dogue store
and corners to top of hill beyond the John G.
Pollock jr farm to the "Hastings Place". Cemetery
is beyond house, but before the first of a series
of trailers.

STAPLES, A. Barbara 1944 – 1945
    Addie Bell d. 7 June 1971 age 85 years 11 months 13 days
    Betty S. Aug 1880 – May 1958
    Charles June 1887 – Feb 1959
    Daniel B. 20 Aug 1895 – 27 Dec 1932
    Ellen Jane 3 May 1857 – 23 Sept 1938
    H. Thomas 1941 – 1950
    Henry Clay 1854 – 6 June 1918
    Henry Clay d. 16 Feb 1953 husb of Lucy S.

STAPLES, Herbert S. 15 May 1923 – 8 June 1951   Vet WW II
   James 14 Dec 1823 – 19 Jan 1873 husb of Sarah Jane, [stone erected by
       their two daughters, Ellen Jan Staples and Mrs. Martha
       Staples Weedon.

   James A. Jan 1876 – Dec 1956
   James T. 1874 – 1948
   Lucy S. d. 1 Feb 1953   wife of Henry C.
   Martha   ... see WEEDON

   Sarah Jane 24 Mar 1818 – 14 Apr 1893 wife of James, [stone erected by
       their two daughters, Ellen Jan Staples and Mrs. Martha
       Staples Weedon.

   Thomas d. 8 Nov 1918 age 72 years
   Virginia 15 Jan 1842 – 29 Aug 1911
   Wayne R. 12 June 1956 – 24 Apr 1957
   William 1866 – 1942

WEEDON, James Buck sr. d. 27 July 1939 age 85 years father, beside Martha S.
   Martha S. 14 Aug 1865 – 6 June 1936 70 years mother, beside James B. sr.

STAPLES FAMILY CEMETERY

        DIRECTIONS: Route 3 East to King George. Across from court-
               house bear right on Route 638 to house on right
               just before the "End of State Maintainence" sign.
               Cemetery is to left rear of house. Note: There
               is also a low concrete block enclosed area
               approximately 8' x 8' with no markers

STAPLES, Benjamin Harrison sr. 7 Dec 1888 – 25 Feb 1970 married 18 Sept 1935
       Name of bride not given.

STAPLES FAMILY CEMETERY

        DIRECTIONS: Route 3 East to King George. Across from court-
               house bear right on Route 638 to private drive
               which turns South just beyond the "End of State
               Maintainence" sign. Note: This cemetery is one
               that was overgrown and without stones when the
               present owners bought. It has been cleared and
               cemetery boundaries marked with four apple trees
               which were planted at the four corners. The
               cemetery is near the house. Informants: owners.

MORGAN, Baby brother and mother of Wm B. Morgan who resides in King George.
STAPLES, other family members. Note Mrs. Morgan was a "Staple".

STUART FAMILY CEMETERY AT SALISBURY

DIRECTIONS: Not given in manuscript by Hugh Roy Stuart.
However, he stated that the farm is now called
CEDAR GROVE Manuscript dated 1962

FOOTE, Sara ... see STUART

GRYMES, Benjamin Custis d. Dec 1930 husb of Rosalie E. Stuart
Rosalie E. Stuart d. 23 Mar 1962 wife of Benjamin Custis Grymes

STUART, Richard son of Wm and Sara Foote Stuart, no dates given
Richard [Dr.] son of Richard, grandson of Rev. Wm and Sara
Rosalie no dates, husb not given, mother of Richard and of Mrs. Rosalie
E. Stuart Grymes
Rosalie E. ... see STUART
Sara Foote no dates wife of Rev. William
William [Rev.] husb of Sara Foote, father of Richard

STUART FAMILY CEMETERY AT FAIR HAVEN

DIRECTIONS: Not given. Information from Hugh Roy Stuart
manuscript of 1962.

GRYMES, Martha Carter ... see STUART

STUART, John Alexander d. 1807
John Alexander died after 1822 husb of Martha Carter Grymes, son of John
Alexander Stuart
Martha Carter Grymes died after 1822 wife of John Alexander

SUTTLE FAMILY CEMETERY

DIRECTIONS: Route 3 East to Route 205 to Route 619 East to
Route 218 North. On right just after turn is an
old two story house. Cemetery is behind the
house in a grove of trees. Very overgrown with
honeysuckle and poison ivy. According to Paul
Slaw there are at least two children here without
tombstones.

SUTTLE, J. Samuel 22 Oct 1870 - 5 Jan 1899 son
Robert V. 29 Aug 1845 - 16 May 1901 husb of Virginia L., father
Virginia L. 20 Mar 1845 - 17 Dec 1916 mother, wife of Robert V.

TALIAFERRO FAMILY CEMETERY

DIRECTIONS: Route 3 East to Route 605 North for 2.6 miles to
              drive on right at bottom of hill. Cemetery is in
              field to left rear of house.

BARBOUR, Lucy Maria 6 Feb 1797 – 15 July 1843 dau of James and Lucy Johnson
              Barbour, married 10 June 1822 to John Seymour
              Taliaferro.

TALIAFERRO, John Seymour 15 Jan 1798 – 4 June 1830   son of John and Lucy
              Hooe Taliaferro, husb of Lucy Maria Barbour. On
              obelisk "To our Parents". [second stone stated :
              "d. 4 June 1830 age 32 years"]

TAYLOE FAMILY CEMETERY

DIRECTIONS: Route 3 East to Route 607 South. At airstrip
              across from Van Der Wert's is the Raymond Guess
              property. May be entered from Route 607 or from
              route 610. Inquire at house about cemetery.
              According to Mr. John G. Pollock jr. it is an
              old TAYLOE FAMILY CEMETERY. Not visited or
              recorded.

TAYLOR FAMILY CEMETERY

DIRECTIONS: Route 3 East to Route 637 South for 0.6 miles to
              end of road. Sign: Frank B. Taylor Mount View
              Farm. Go through gate, across cattle guard. At
              0.8 miles cross second cattle guard. Inquire at
              house for permission and directions. Laura Taylor
              informant.

BURNLEY, Mary Wilkins ... see TAYLOR

OVERTON, Lilly ... see TAYLOR

TAYLOR, Benjamin Temple 26 Aug 1872 – 27 Feb 1969
        Hardin Burnley 14 Dec 1858 – 29 July 1870
        Lilly Overton 23 June 1877 – 23 May 1967
        Mary Wilkins Burnley 2 May 1832 – 3 Jan 1899 wife of William R.
        Wilkins B. 31 Dec 1874 – 5 Jan 1949
        William Robinson 11 April 1830 – 23 Dec 1900 husb of Mary Wilkins
                          Burnley

THAYER FAMILY CEMETERY

DIRECTIONS: Route 617 East from Route 301 to Route 633 South
for 0.01 miles. Cemetery is on right behind the
J.P.Thayer farmhouse. Fenced, neat, well kept.

THAYER, Edith M. 27 Feb 1868 – 26 May 1932

THORNTON CEMETERY AT SOCIETY HILL

DIRECTIONS: Information from 1962 manuscript of Hugh Roy
Stuart.

THORNTON, _____ wife of Francis, mother of John and William
    Francis b. 21 July 17_5   date of death not given. father of John and Wm

WASHINGTON FAMILY CEMETERY AT POTOMAC VIEW

DIRECTIONS: Information from 1962 manuscript of Hugh Roy
Stuart.

WASHINGTON, John Hooe   died 1830   husband of two wives

WELCH FAMILY CEMETERY

DIRECTIONS: Route 3 East to Route 205 East to Mt Lebanon Farm
on left. It is the first large white house beyond
Route 617 on your left. Large barns, ballfield,
tennis courts, etc. visible from road. Permission
and further directions needed. There are five
wooden markers and possibly other graves in addition to those recorded.

"B.A." footstone
"M. S. A." footstone
ASHTON, Elizabeth Jackson ... see WELCH
    Baby   no dates   beside Elizabeth Jackson Ashton Welch
COAKLEY, Irene ... see WELCH
WELCH, Elizabeth Jackson Ashton 5 April 1838 – 11 June 1904 wife of Sylvester
                Morgan Welch
    Irene Coakley 9 Dec 1887 – 30 July 1971 wife of Sylvester B.

WELCH, Sylvester no dates Co A 7 Va Cav CSA husb of Elizabeth Jackson Ashton
Sylvester Burditt 2 June 1874 – 5 Aug 1956 husb of Irene C.

WEST FAMILY CEMETERY

DIRECTIONS: Route 3 East to Route 205 East to Route 218 North
to Route 656 East. Cemetery is in woods across
from Thomas D. Cobb home. Thomas D. Cobb, informant.

WEST, Anna died around 1935 no marker
other family members

INDEX

"B. A." 63

"M.S.A." 63

ACORS
Elizabeth 5

ACRES
J.T. 5

ADKINS
Annie L. 28
Benjamin W. 28
Louisa K. 28

AGAR
Jane 41

ALEXANDER
Ann 18
Catherine Graham 28
Gustavus Brown 20, 22
John 28
Judith Ball Blackburn 20, 22
Marie Heber 20
Sarah Blair Stuart 20 , 22

ALLEN
A. M. 9
Elizabeth W. 5
Jas S. 10
Robert H. 5
Wm J. 5
Wm Sanford 10

ANDERSON
Anne C. 6

ARMSTRONG
Elizabeth Dishman 14
Henry S. 14
Lena 14

ARNOLD
Austina Nelson 29
Bettie 26
Catherine Brockenbrough 29
Charles 29
Elizabeth Goddess 29
Frances B. Price 29
Francis 29
Isaac 29
James 29
Jane 29
Jane Humphries 29
Jemima 29
John 29, 30
John Humphries 29
Lucy 29
Martha 29
Mary 29
Mary Frances 29
Mary Gray 29
Mary Randolph B. 29
Minnie Branche Coghill 29
Sarah Ann 29
Sarah B. 29
Sarah Buckner 29
Thomas 29

ARNOLD
Thomas Randolph 29
Thomas Thornton 29
William 29

ASHBY
Mary 31

ASHTON
Arthur 20
Baby 63
Benjamin 30
Betty Washington Lewis 20, 21, 22
Ella 20
Elizabeth Jackson 63
Fielding Lewis 20, 21
George A. 53
George D. 30
H.D. 15
Lewis Alexander 20, 21
Lucy 21, 53
Lucy Pratt 21
Martha A. 30
Martha Stuart 15
Martha Thornton 37
Mary Barnes Hooe 20, 21
Ruth 21
Wm A.G.D. 20, 21

ATWELL
Mary Alice 26

AUSTIN
Frank 51
Virginia 51

BABER
Emma 58
Thomas B. 58
Thomas B. B. 58

BAILEY
Henry 14

BAKER
Bettie Arnold 26
Susanna 36
Wm Edwards sr 26

BARBOUR
James 62
Lucy Johnson 62
Lucy Maria 62
Philippa 15

BARNES
Lucy 15
Sarah 18

BARTLETT
Lydia Jane 52

BAXTER
Lizzett V. 12
W. H. sr 12

BEALE
Emma Baber 58

BEALE
Genevieve Garnett 58
Richard Channing 58

BECKWITH
Maria 18

BERNARD
Alfred N. 15
Margaret B. M. 15
Margaret Boyd Mason 15

BERRY
Ann Grymes 21
Charles A. 21
Clara T. 31
E. 31
Ella A. 21
Ella Ashton 21
Henry Thacker 21
Jane 21
John 21, 31
Laura 21
Leonard 31
Lucy Ashton 21
Mary 31
Mildred 21
Rebecca Johnson 21
Roberta 21
Thomas M. 21
Virginia 21
Vivian Pratt 21
William P. 21

BILLINGSLEY
Addison Poindexter 31
Almira V. 31
Donnie G. Treakle 31
Ella Johnson 31
Elizabeth J. 31
Gertrude G. 31
James A. 31
Jane 31
Jane Herndon 31
Jos A. [Rev.] 31
Joseph A. 31
Julia E. 31
Kitty 31
Laura Ellen 31
Laura Jane 31
Lewis 32
Lula 32
Sallie 32
Willantina R. Taylor 32
William K. 32

BLACKBURN
Judith Ball 21

BOGGS
Inf. dau. 15
James Henry 15
Lucy 15
Lucy Fitzhugh Grymes Hooe 15
Sallie Withers 26
Thos H. [Rev.] 26

BOOTH
Catherine 19

BOOTH
Mary 19
Thomas 19

BOWIE
Henrietta C. 6
Lucy Michial 6
Rebecca F. 12

BOWLER
C.S. 7
Ellen 8
Emily 8
Minnie 8
Wm M. 8

BOYKIN
Richard Oscar 40
Sally Hudson 40

BRADSHAW
R. B. 6

BRANHAM
Seab 57

BRENT
Lindora 2

BRITTON
Florence Garnett 58

BROKENBOROUGH
Lucy 45
Mary Randolph 29

BROOKS
Barney 10
Carrie Clift 10
Louis J. [Rev.] 27

BROWN
Allie Weedon 44
Belle 58
Daisy D. Lucas 44
Edward D. 48
Eugene 2
Henry 48
Joshan M. 26
Lucy D. 48
Martha 30
Minnie Dickinson 15
Nannie 26
Nannie Stone 21
Raymond 44
W.M. [Rev.] 12
Wm S. 26
William W. 15

BROWNLEY
Hazel 8

BRUCE
Ira Dana 32
James R. 32
Julia Ann 32
Lucy 32
Lucy J. 49
Robert J. 49
Sallie 12
Sallie L. 32
William C. 32
William Julia 32

BUCKLEY
Ida 9

BUMBRY
Galvia W. 33
George 33
Mary E. 33
Richard 33

BURCHE
William Chase 37

BURGESS
Roland A. 33
Viola S. 33

BURNLEY
Mary Wilkins 62

CAMPBELL
Pearl 34
Reverend 34

CARPENTER
Edmonia 12
John H. 12
Nannie B. 12
Son 12
William H. 14

CARUTHERS
Azeele Hersey 34
Carrie L. Ninde 34
Edwin Clark 34
Veolo Oglesby [M.D.] 34

CARVER
Annie L. 3
F. 9
J. 9
John T. 3
L. A. 9
W. A. 8

CATLETT
Rosalie 21

CATO
Lucy Boggs 15

CHINAULT
M. J. [Mrs.] 10

CLARK
Ollie 24

CLARKE
Julier Augusta 36
Robert 36

CLIFT
Carrie 10
James 6
Marias 10
Pearl 40

CLOPTON
Alice B. 35
Elcy 35
Ella 35

COAKLEY
Cora 47
Daniel W. 12
Ginny 52
Harry B. 12
Julia Potts 54
Mary Ellen 8
Mary Piper 54
Nancy 11
Richard Powell 54
Irene 63

COAKLEY
Sarah A. 12
Wm Bevan 54

COBB
Thomas 35
Thomas D. 35, 44
William 35

COLLIER
Arthur S. 35
Sallie B. 35
Thomas M. 35

COLLINS
Chas. Read [Col.] 15
Roy M. 15
Susan Augusta 15

COLTON
Anna H. Saunders 15
Anna Madison 15
Nina B. 15
William 15

CONWAY
Katherine 12

CUSTIS
Ellen 45

DADE
Elizabeth P. 21
Francis 18

DARLING
Charles Tiernan 45
Nancy 45
Virginia Gertrude 45

DAVIS
Bettie 24
John G. 24
Lloyd 27
Lucy F. 24
M.V. 24
Reuben 24
W.H. 24

DeSHAZO
Edward 12
Laura Ann 12
Minnie N. 36
W. H. 36

DICKENS
Ginny 55

DICKERSON
Family 30

DICKINSON
Ada Virginia 4
Attie Maria 45
Estelle Lewis 45
John Saunders 45
Mary Imogen 45
Minnie 15
Osceola G. 45
Virginia Gertrude 45

DILLARD
Ellen Ann 12
James Lee 12

DISHMAN
Addison T. 36

DISHMAN
Anne Edmonds Jones 36
Asbury C. 36
Elizabeth 14
Jennie 36
John 36
John T. 36
Julia C. 36
M. R. 36
Mary Jane 36
Samuel 36
Susanna Baker 36

DODD
Alexander 10
John 10

DOHERTY
Nannie S. Brown 26
Wm J. 26

DRINKARD
Marion W. 21
Thomas 21

DUFFY
Patrick 21

EDWARDS
Lloyd B. 37
Lucie B. 37
Lucy E. 37

ELKINS
Charles Barbour 6
Monimia Augusta 6

EMERSON
Belle 54
Mary 53

FARMER
Charles Nicholas 12
Edith Walker 12
Gertrude H. 12
Julia B. 13
Nicholas 13
Wm M. 13

FERRELL
Ann 38
Delphia A. 9
Elizabeth Gray 38
J. A. 9
J. H. 9
James A. 38
James Austin sr 38
Lucy J. 38
Mildred 13
Murney I. 38
W. 9

FINNALL
Eliza 11
James 11

FISHER
Eliz 24, 25
Eliza 55

FITZHUGH [Fitz-Hugh]
Alice 19
Catherine 19
Caroline P. Turner 21
Carrie Alice 21, 22
Drury Bolling 21, 22
Elizabeth 20

FITZHUGH [Fitz-Hugh]
Francis C. [Dr.] 20
Francis Conway 21, 22
Henry 19 , 20
Henry Stith 21, 22
Jane Berry 21, 22
Jane Charlotte Washington 4
Lola Ruggles 22
Louisa Conway 18, 19
Marcellus T. 8
Rosa Spence 20
Sarah A. McDaniel 8
Susannah 20
Thomas 19

FOOTE
Sara 61

FORLOINES
Matilda Lee 13

FOSTER
Lucian M. 41
Nannie I 41

FRANK
Allie Bertha 43
Bernard G. 43
Jeremiah A. 43
William B. 31

FREELAND
Elizabeth 16

GAINEY
Zachariah [Rev.] 7

GALLAHAN
M. R. 6

GARBER
Joseph Martin 24, 25
Mary Elizabeth 24, 25
Nancy Jane Strickler 24, 25

GARNER
Agnes 33

GARNETT
Algernon S. [M.D.] 58
Belle 58
Belle Brown 58
Emma 58
Emma L. 58
Florence 58
Henry T. 58
John 58
Josephine 58
Josephine Ijams 58
Laura Hayward 58
Miyoko 58
Stuart Bankhead 58
Thomas Baber 58
Thomas S. 58
Thomas Stuart 58
Thomas Stuart jr 58
Wm B. 58

GARRETT
Mary E. 10
Reuben 10

GOERLITZ
Cari 49
Emelie 49
Henry 49
Marie 49

GOODE
Benjamin 22
Genevieve Gouldman 22

GOODING
Annie V. Grigsby 13

GOODMAN
Mr. & Mrs. 38

GOULDMAN
Arthur Stainback 22
Bessie Taylor 22
Emmett Jesse 22
Florence B. 32
Genevieve 22
George Jesse 22
Harold Moore 22
Ida Stainback 22
J. Walter 32
Robert Henry 22
Ruth Ashton 22

GRAHAM
Catherine 28

GRAVATT
Robert 6
Walter 6

GRAY
Caroline V. 24
Ira Franklin 24
Lucy Quesenberry 24

GREEN
Annie Pearl 39
Bettie 56
Daphnie 56
Delda 56
Erasmus 56
James Leven 39
John B. 39
Levven J. 39
Mary A. 56
Mary Imogen 45
Nannie J. 39
Wesley L. 39

GREENE
Callie 46
Howard 47
Virginia 47

GREER
Nancy Jane 42

GREGAN
Robert 34

GREGORY
A. G. 35

GRIFFI
James 2

GRIFFIN
Martha 11

GRIFFITHS
———— 39

GRIGSBY
Annie V. 13
Baily L. 13
George W. [Capt.] 6
Hunter E. 24

GRIGSBY
  J. Cleveland 24
  Katherine Conway 13
  Marcess S. 11
  Mary L. 11
  Rebecca F. Bowie 13
  William E. 13
  William Franklin 24

GROSS
  Albert Franz 47, 48
  Catherine 48
  Lucie McKenney 48
  Lucy Virginia 47

GRYMES
  Ann 22
  Ann Eilbeck Mason 19
  Ann Nicholas 19
  Benjamin [Capt.] 19
  Benjamin jr 37
  Benjamin Custis 61
  Benjamin Richard 22
  Edmonia 37
  Elizabeth 16
  Elizabeth Hansford 22
  Family 21, 22
  George Edmund 22
  George Nicholas 19
  Helen Virginia "Vickie" 45
  Kate 22
  Lucy Fitzhugh 18
  Lucy Lewis 45
  Martha Carter 61
  Martha Thornton Ashton 37
  Mary 22
  R. Carter N. 45
  Rebecca Johnson 22
  Robert Carter Nicholas 37
  Rosalie E. Stuart 61
  Wm Fitzhugh 37

GUESS
  Raymond 62

"V. T. H." 26

HAENECHE
  Johanna 22
  Rudolph 22

HALL
  Rosa 31
  Sarah Frances 50

HANSFORD
  Elizabeth 22

HARGEST
  Anna Stinger 16
  Thomas Jefferson 16

HARRELL
  Wilbur Rollins [Mrs.] 55, 49

HARRIS
  Annie King 39
  Beatrice 33
  Clyde B. 39
  Herby F. 10
  Isabelle Mason 39
  Melvin 33
  Thomas Baldwin 39

HARRISON
  Inf. twins 18
  Mary A. 18

HAWKINS
  Maude 51

HAYES
  Charles Martin 8
  Charlotte Moyer 26
  Hettie Mabel 8
  Isiah F. 26
  Josiah 8
  Sarah L. 8

HAYWARD
  Laura 58

HEFLIN
  Eleanor 32
  Horace Ashton 32
  James O. 32
  Jane Billingsley 32
  Lula Billingsley 32
  Robert Ashby 32
  William Lewis 32
  William Nelson 32

HENDERSON
  Eli M. 11
  Elizabeth 11
  Elizabeth Acors 6
  G. Milton 6
  George T. 6
  Horace 6
  Infants [six] 6
  Jas L. 6
  Julia A. 6
  Julia B. 6
  Leonard Merrell 40
  Lizzie 6
  Martha A.L. 40
  Mary A. 11
  Mary M. 11
  Nancy H. 6
  Oliver Maxwell 40
  Otis 11
  Sarah Jane 6
  Wm H. 6
  Wm J. 6
  Wm Merrell 40

HENNINGS
  Ann 28, 29

HERNDON
  Benjamin T. 6
  Bernice 6
  James B. 6
  Jane 32
  Meredith T. 6
  Nettie M. 6
  Oranel 6

HOMOISELLE
  Caroline 22

HOOE
  Abram Barnes 18, 19, 20
  Ann Alexander 18
  Arthur Edward 18
  Caroline Johnson 18
  Charles Thomas 18
  Elizabeth Grymes 16
  Frances Fitzhugh 18
  Frances Townsend 18
  George Mason 16
  Gerard 18
  Gerard Seymour 18
  Horatio Rinaldo 18
  Isaac Foote 16, 22

HOOE
  John [Capt.] 18, 19
  John Thomas 19
  Louisa Conway Fitzhugh 18, 19
  Lucy 62
  Lucy Barnes 16, 22
  Lucy Fitzhugh Grymes 16, 17,
           18, 19
  Lucy Fitzhugh 19
  Mary A. 19
  Mary Barnes 21, 22
  Mary Grymes 22
  Medora Boyd 15, 16
  Rice 18, 19, 22
  Robert Arthur 15, 16
  Sarah Barnes 18, 19
  Sarah Hornwood Johnson 18,
           19
  Seymour [Mrs.] 19
  William Fitzhugh 19
  Xarifa Mason 16

HOOSER
  Flora M. 54

HOWARD
  John Lewis 36
  Kate R. 36

HOWE
  James Phillip 22

HUDSON
  Blanche A. 40
  Charlie Carlton 40
  Frank Temple sr 40
  G. R. 40
  Gladys 40
  Mary F. 40
  Pearl Clift 40
  R. H. 40
  Sally 40
  Vickie 40

HUGHES
  Julia A. Smith 13
  Samuel 14

HUMPHRIES
  Jane 29

HUNTER
  Frederick G.S. 16
  Henry H. 16
  Rose T. 4
  Susan Rose Turner 16

INSCOE
           41
  Charles H. 41
  Cordelia 10
  Earnest 38
  H.J. 41
  Ida 41
  J.F. 10
  James M. 41
  Jane Agar 41
  Mary 38
  Mollie V. 41
  W. J. 41
  William H. 41

JACKSON
  R. R. 24
  Rufus 41

JENKINS
  Horace 42
  Malinda 10
  Robert P. 10
  Thadeus 6

JENNINGS
  Mr. 38, 41, 42

JETT
  Carrie Turner 4
  Ethel Newton 4
  Hallie Mitchell 4
  Virginia Mitchell 4
  Wm N. 4

JOHNSON
  Beanoil 1
  Ella 32
  Horatio 19
  Katie B. 33
  Lucy 62
  Rebecca 22
  Sarah Hornwood 18, 19
  Will 35
  Willia H. 33

JOHNSTON
  Nancy Jane Greer 42
  Philip Potts 42

JONES
  Anne C. Anderson 6
  Anne Edmonds 36
  Ashton 6
  Belle 11
  Elizabeth L. Payne 8
  Gordon 6
  Infant daughter 6
  J. Frank 8
  James E. 36
  Julia A. 24
  Julia C.D. 36
  Lucie M. 6
  Maria C. 26
  Myrtle 6
  Ollie Clark 24
  Prigie A. 6
  Robert M. 6
  Sidney 11
  Weston B. sr 24

KEARNEY
  Kate 16

KING
  A. 8
  A. Dorsey Rollins 56
  Annie 39
  Annie Wave 56
  Daughter 25
  D. Guy 56
  E.F. 56
  Eliza Bet 56
  Eliza Fisher 25, 56
  Ivy Moss 25
  James Bagby 56
  Jennette A. 25, 56
  Mary Ella 25
  Mary Syndor 56
  Sarah Adeline 8
  Thomas 56
  Thomas S. 25
  Vivian 56
  William Ellsworth 56
  William H. 25, 56
  Zoe 56

KINZER
  Ernest T. 35
  Grace 35
  Nocie 35

KNOTT
  Lloyd Wm 40

KRIEGSTEDT
  A. Fredric 49
  August 49
  August H. 49
  Joseph 49
  Oscar 49
  Pauline M. 49

LANGLEY
  Charles 6
  Martha E. 6

LEE
  Alice 10
  Almira R. 25
  Annie Mildred 46
  Annie T. 10
  Cora Olinda 47
  Eldred 25, 43
  Hannah 23
  Howard 25
  Ira Franklin 25
  Ivy Moss King 25
  Joseph 10
  Mary A. 25, 43
  Mary Elizabeth Garber 24,
    25
  Mary Ella King 25
  Mary M. 43
  Thomas 46
  Thomas Eldred sr 25

LEWIS
  Alice A. Tayloe 51
  Attaway Miller 45
  Attie Maria 45
  Betty Washington 21, 22
  Catherine 45
  Dangerfield 42, 45
  Edgar V. 45
  Ellen Custis 45
  Estelle 45
  Fielding 45
  George Washington 45
  Helen Zola 45
  Henry Byrd 43
  Jane B. 45
  Katie D. 45
  Lucy 45
  Lucy B. 45
  Mary I. 45, 46
  Mary Imogen Green 45
  Mary Washington 45
  Mary Willis 45
  Samuel D. 45
  T. M. [Dr.] 51

LOCKE
  Belle 5

LOW
  Joseph Hooker 51
  Maude Hawkins 51

LUCAS
  Clarence 44
  Daisy D. 44
  Harry Stuart 44
  Kate 44

LUCAS
  Lilly [Lillie] 44
  Nancy J. 44
  Phil 44

LUNSFORD
  Georgiana 44
  Nancy Potts 44
  Robertine T. 44
  Wm Potts 44

MARBLE
  Jennifer Lynn 40
  Vickie Hudson 40

MARSHALL
  Anna M. 46
  Annie Mildred 46
  Howard sr 46
  Howard Kirk jr 46
  John Wyatt 46
  Rush 25
  S. J. 9
  Samuel 25
  Susan J. 25
  Thomas L. sr 46
  Wee 36

MARTIN
  Ida Tolson 37

MASON
  Ann Eilbeck 19
  Beverly W. 16
  C. 16
  Charles 16
  Charles Anna 46
  Charles T. 16
  E. F. 16
  E. W. 16
  Ellen 16
  Elizabeth Freeland 16
  Enoch 16
  Eugine 16
  Henry Alan 16
  Isabelle 39
  Jefferson Randolph 16
  John E. 16
  Julian J. 16
  Kate Kearney 16
  Lucy Roy 16
  Margaret Boyd 15, 16
  Maria Jefferson 16
  Mari[s] Randolph 46
  Octavia 16
  Sidnie A. 16
  Susan Augusta 16
  Susan Taylor 15, 16
  W. Cary N. 16
  Wiley Roy 15, 16

MATHESON
  Addie Elizabeth Nave 50

McCLANAHAN
  Patsy 47

McDANIEL
  Lucy 47
  Mr & Mrs 34
  Sarah A. 8

McDONIEL
  Callie 47
  D. 47
  George Culver 47
  Hallie T. 47

McDONIEL
    William 47

McDOWNEY
    Ernest 43
    Mary Emma 43

McGUIRE
    Edward B. [Rev.] 4
    Jane 4
    Marie Heber Alexander 22
    William [Rev.] 22

McKENNE
    W. H. 9

McKENNEY
    Alice 53
    Alice B. 47
    Ann Mariah 47
    Cora Olinda Lee 47
    Elizabeth 49
    Elizabeth Quesenberry 47
    George 53
    George Brown 47, 49
    George C. 47, 49
    George Crabb 47
    George L. 48
    Georgie 48
    Grandma 54
    Henry [Harry] 47
    Ida 48, 53
    James C. 48
    James Larkin 47, 54
    James S. 47
    John Quesenberry 47
    Lillo [Lills] Vondell 47
    Lucy Virginia 47
    Madline H. 48
    Mariah Louisa 47, 49
    Mary 47
    Mary Elizabeth 47
    Mary Frances Price 54
    Mary L. 47
    Patricia McClanahan 47, 49
    Sarah E. 47
    Wm A. 47, 49
    William H. 47
    William Q. 47

MERRYMAN
    Eugene W. 13
    Fannie N. 13
    J.P. 13
    Mother 13
    Russell G. 13

MIFFLETON
    D.W. 49
    Ella 13
    Forest O. 49
    Rosalie 49

MILLER
    Henry 24

MILLS
    Emma Garnett 58

MINOR
    Hassetline C. 26
    John T. 26
    Sallie A. 26

MITCHELL
    Virginia 4

MONTGOMERY
    Elizabeth Frances 29
    Robert Hall 29
    Sarah B. 29

MORGAN
    Baby brother 60
    Esther Darleen 50
    Fenton 50
    George F. 50
    Glenn Edward 50
    J. H. 50
    James Wm 11
    L. V. 50
    Lorena 50
    Mother 60
    Nannie B. 50
    Nellie 26
    Pemmie 26
    Robert Lawson 50
    Rudolphus 50
    Sanford A. 26
    William B. 60
    Winfield F. 50

MOUNTJOY
    Clifford A. 16
    Jemima 16
    Phillis 16
    William [Capt.] 16

MOYER
    Charlotte 26

MULLEN
    John Henry 13
    Maria 13
    Mary Jane 13

MUNSELL
    Addison T. 17
    Catherine E. 17

MURPHY
    Wm H. 11

MUSE
    Sallie J. 26
    William S. 26

NASH
    and SLAW 7, 51

NAVE
    Addie Elizabeth 50
    Beulah D. 50
    Grace M. 50
    Henry Thomas 50
    Homer 50
    Omey 50
    Richard Roderick 50
    Roderick Samuel B. 50
    Tabitha Maude 50
    Theodore R. 50

NEWBILL
    John Horace [Rev.] 25
    Mollie Parker 25

NETHERTON
    Elizabeth 20
    Henry 20

NEWTON
    Fannie B. 9
    Harlan W. 40
    James B. 9

NEWTON
    Lucy M. 13
    Robert 13

NICHOLAS
    Ann 19
    Jane 16

NINDE
    Carrie L. 34
    F. Fairfax [M.D.] 22, 23
    Genevieve A. 22
    Lucy Pratt Ashton 22, 23

OLIVE
    Clara M. 14
    George A. 14
    Joseph H. 14
    Mary J. 14
    Nicholis N. 14
    Thomas W. 14

OVERTON
    Lilly 62

OWEN
    Wm M. 6

OWENS
    Bennie 1
    Mary S. 11
    Wm W. [Rev.] 11

PARKER
    John 11
    Mollie 25
    Peyton 25
    Wm H. 25

PARR
    Dean 33
    G. I. 33
    J. W. 33

PATRICK
    Mable Valorie 33

PAYNE
    Agnes C. 13
    Alice B. 48
    Elizabeth L. 8
    Minor M. 13
    N.F. 47, 48
    Patrick H. 13

PAYTON
    Harvey 59

PEED
    Ginny Coakley 52
    Jennie 11
    John N. 11, 52
    Nancy Powell 11

PEYTON
    Arthur L. 44
    Benjamin 44
    Carrie E. 52
    J.F. 52
    Lilly Lucas 44
    Randolph 52
    Rose 44

PHILLIPS
    George Bruce 48
    Georgie McKenney 48, 53,
        54

PIPER
  Mary 54

PITTS
  Bessie M. 52, 53
  Lewis 52, 53
  Raymond 53
  Thomas C. 53

POLLOCK
  Estelle Lewis 45, 46
  Infant son 45
  John G. jr 30, 59, 62
  John Gray 45, 46, 53
  Katie D. Lewis 45, 46
  Matthew B. 45, 46
  Minnie Gertrude Smith 53

POTTS
  Alexander 8
  Fannie B. 54
  Hezekiah 36
  Jennie Dishman 36
  Julia 54
  Mary Ellen Coakley 8
  Nancy 44

POUNDS
  Bruce 41
  Ida Inscoe 41

POWELL
  Fielding L. 46
  Nancy 11

PRATT
  Lucy 23
  Murnie E. 6
  Vivian 23

PRICE
  Abner Buckner 47
  Algee 55
  Belle Emerson 54
  Benjamin F. 8
  Bettie B. 54
  Frances B. 30
  George W. 54
  Ginny Dickens Rollins 55
  Lucy Ashton 53
  Lucy McDaniel 47
  Martin Luther 53
  Mary Emerson 54
  Mary Frances 54
  Walter 54
  Wm B. K. [Dr.] 54

PURKS
  Charles T. 13
  Daniel 13
  Ella 13
  Ella Jane 13
  Ella Miffleton 13
  John Lee 13
  Judith 13
  Matilda Lee Forloines 13
  Sallie Bruce 13
  Vannie May 13

QUESENBERRY
  Alice B. 48
  Elizabeth 48
  Lucy 25
  Monimia 37
  William O. 1

RANDOLPH
  Jane Nicholas 16
  Maria Jefferson 17
  Mari[s] 46
  Thomas Jefferson 16

RATCLIFFE
  Cleland K. 1
  Ethel A. 39
  S. A. 26
  Thomas M. 26

RAWLETT
  C. H. 49
  Martha 49

READ [Reed]
  John. 54

REAMY
  Alexander 11
  Anna Staples 11

RICE
  S.B. [Rev.] 13

ROBB
  Anna Augusta 4
  Nancy Darling 45
  R. L. 4

ROCK
  Mary A. 25

ROGERS
  Charles W. 26
  James E. 8
  Margaret E. 26
  Marie Elois 13
  William J. 13
  William Larence 13

ROLLINS
  A. Dorsey 56
  Albert B. 55
  Ann L. 8
  Annie Belle 55
  Bettie Green 56
  Ferdinand 13
  Ginny 55
  Jennette A. 25, 56
  Joseph Wilbur 55
  Kirk 55
  Lovell B. 56
  Mary 13
  Patsy 55
  Sidney A. Rose 55
  William 55
  William B. 8
  Winford 55

ROSE
  Alexander M. 4
  Anna 4
  Catherine Corbin Taliaferro
      17
  Collier [Mrs.] 54
  F.S. 4
  Martha Griffin 11
  Mary C. L. 25
  Rose T. Hunter 4
  Sidney A. 55
  William Augustine 4

ROY
  Lucy 16

RUGGLES
  Lola 23

RUSSELL
  Joseph A. [Rev.] 23
  Joseph Parker 23
  Sarah E. 23

SAUNDERS
  Anna H. 17

SCOTT
  David 8
  Hazel Brownley 8
  Laura 8

SHANKLIN
  Anna G. 27

SHELTON
  Agnes Garner 33
  Esther B. 56
  Gordon W. 56
  J.S. 56
  John Fred 56
  Lena B. 56
  Lenor D. 56
  Luke M. 56
  Margaret D.L. 56
  Matt L. 56
  Sarah A. 56
  Virginia B. 56

SLAW
  Paul 51

SMITH
  Ada Virginia Dickinson 4
  Albert Turner 4
  Augustine [Dr.] 16
  C. B. [Rev.] 2
  Caroline Alice 4
  Julia A. 14
  Minnie Gertrude 53
  Susan Taylor 16, 17

SNYDER
  Anna G. 25
  H. J. 25

SORRELL
  Brother 57
  C.H. 57
  Father 57
  George W. 14
  George W. [Mrs.] 9
  Lizzie 57
  Mildred Ferrell 14
  Mother 57

SPENCE
  Rosa 20

SPILLMAN
  Benjamin J. 26
  Lucy B. 26
  Maria C. Jones 26
  Mary Alice Atwell 26
  Wm Lansdown 26

SPILMAN
  Mary L. 57

STAINBACK
  Ida 22, 23

STAPLES
  A. Barbara   59
  Addie Bell   59
  Alvin J.   59
  Anna   11
  Baby girl   59
  Benjamin Harrison sr   60
  Betty S.   59
  Charles   59
  Daniel B.   59
  Ellen Jane   59
  Ellen Jan [Mrs.]   60
  Eva Etta   59
  Francis C.   59
  H. Thomas   59
  Henry Clay   59
  Herbert S.   60
  James   60
  James A.   60
  James T.   60
  Lucy S.   60
  Martha   60
  Milton Turner sr   59
  Norman S.   59
  Roy   28
  Sarah Jane   60
  Thomas   60
  Virginia   60
  Wayne R.   60
  William   60

STEWART
  Edmund Lee   23
  Hannah Lee   23
  James Van Dyme   23
  K.J. [Rev.]   23

STINGER
  Anna   17

STONE
  Nannie   23

STRICKLER
  Nancy Jane   25

STROTHER
  Carolyn   40
  George Edwin sr   40
  Gorgetta   5
  John Thornton   40
  Kate C.   5
  M. E.   40
  Minnie   5

STUART
  Hugh Roy   30, 52, 53, 61,
    63
  John Alexander   61
  Martha   17
  Martha Carter Grymes   61
  Richard   61
  Rosalie   61
  Rosalie E.   61
  Sarah Blair   23
  Sara Foote   61
  William [Rev.]   61

SUMNER
  Allen M.   1

SUTTLE
  Daisy   14
  J. Samuel   61
  Robert V.   61
  Virginia L.   61

SYNDOR
  Mary   56

TALIAFERRO
  Belle Garnett   58
  Edwin Maywood   58
  John   62
  John Seymour   62
  Lucy Hooe   62
  Lucy Maria Barbour   62

TATE
  George Dewey   40

TAYLOE
  Alice A.   51
  Charles   51
  Edward Thornton   17
  George Ogle   17
  John V[fifth]   46
  Mary   17
  Mary Ogle   17
  Mary Willis Lewis   46

TAYLOR
  Belle Locke   5
  Benjamin Temple   62
  Bessie   22, 23
  Charles H.   25
  Frank B.   62
  Hardin Burnley   62
  Jane E.   25
  John   5
  Laura   62
  Lilly Overton   62
  Mary Wilkins Burnley   62
  Wilkins B.   62
  Willantina R.   32
  William Robinson   62

TENNENT
  Jane S.   27
  Roberta Berry   21, 23

THAYER
  Edith M.   63
  J. P.   63

THOMAS
  Charles   33
  Martha   33

THORNTON
  Cecelia P. Washington   23
  Francis   63
  John   63
  Wade A.   23
  William   63

THURSTON
  Thomas H.   37

TOLSON
  Edmonia Grymes   37
  Forresta T.   37
  Francis Annesly   37
  Ida   37
  Thomas H.   37
  Thomas H. jr   37

TOWNSEND
  Frances   19
  Robert   18, 19

TREAKLE
  Donnie G.   32

TRICKER
  Baby   31
  Charlotte   31
  Clara T. Berry   31
  D. C.   31
  Daniel F.   31
  Jesse V.   31
  Rosa Hall   31
  Russell S.   31
  Sarah   31
  Tabitha   31

TRIGGER
  C.   6
  H.   6
  J.   6
  L.   7
  M.   7
  Stanfield   7

TURNER
  Anna Augusta   5
  Caroline Alice Smith   5
  Caroline P.   23
  Carolinus   4, 5, 16
  Carrie   5
  Elizabeth   5
  Evelyn   5
  George   5
  Harry   5
  Henry Vivion   4, 5
  Jane Charlotte Washington
    Fitzhugh   5
  Jane McGuire   5
  Margaret Locke   5
  Mary Lee   5
  Richard Vivion   5
  Susan A.   4, 5
  Susan Rose   16, 17
  William Smith   5

TYLER
  Arthur L.   10
  Bennie   10
  Eddie   10
  Louis   10
  Sallie   10
  W. H.   12

VAN DER WERT
  Bert   43, 62

VAN NESS
  Francis   55

VON DELL
  Lillo [Lills]   48

WALKER
  Ames   2
  E.E.   27
  Edith   14
  Edwin O.   14
  Elizabeth   20
  George W.   7
  J.L.   14
  Kathleen   27
  Mary A.   14
  Mary D. Wallace   7
  R.   14
  Rubie   27
  S. L.   14
  Sallie Esther   27
  William   20

WALLACE
  Arthur W.   14

WALLACE
  Mary D. 7

WARING
  Rosalie V. 51
  Thomas R. 51
  W.L. 51

WASHINGTON
  Caroline Homoiselle 23
  Cecelia P. 23
  Henry T. 23
  John Hooe 63
  Lucinda 23
  Marion 23
  Rosalie Catlett 23
  Virginia 23
  Wm Henry 21, 23

WATTS
  Robert [Rev.] 7

WAVE
  Annie 56

WEEDON
  Bettie L. 56
  James Buck sr 60
  Martha S. 60
  W. A. 56

WELCH
  Elizabeth Jackson Ashton
     63, 64
  Irene Coakley 63, 64
  Sylvester 63, 64
  Sylvester Burditt 63, 64

WEST
  Anna 64

WHITE
  Bernard Ashby 32
  Bettie Davis 25
  Bettie M. 2
  Frank 2
  Isaiah 2
  John B. 8
  Mary Ashby 32
  Robert Ashby 32
  Sallie Billingsley 32
  Thos L. 25

WIESKLKLAD
  Alma 49
  Franz 49

WILEY
  Lucy Roy 16

WILKERSON
  Myrtle L. 44

WILKINS
  Bush 14
  Daisy Suttle 14
  Lena Armstrong 14

WILLIAMS
  Eliza 7
  Gertrude V. 33

WILSON
  Burnett 24
  Pauline 24

WISTO __
  Marie Louise 24
  ——— 24

WITHERS
  Sallie 27
  John 18

WOLFE
  Mary P. 17
  P. T. F. 17

WORRELL
  Malcolm 1
  Willie [Miss.] 23

ZOLA
  Helen 46

[__]LASS
  F.M. 8
  Lota 8

Watch 47

INDEX OF PLACES

Washington, D.C. 27

MARYLAND
  Ann Arundel County 19
  Baltimore 26

VIRGINIA
  Albemarle County 16
  Essex County 8, 56
  Spotsylvania Courthouse 15
  Stafford 16
  Westmoreland County 3, 7,
        14, 22, 39
Locations In KING GEORGE
  Ambar 5
  King George Courthouse 1,
        15, 26, 40
  Muddy Creek 9
  Ninde 7, 54
  Owens 9, 11, 40
  Port Conway 4
  Rollins Fork 25, 55

CHURCHES
  Grant's Hill Baptist Church in
        Westmoreland 7
  Greenmount in Baltimore 26
  Peoples Union Baptist Church
        of Washington, D.C.
        27
  Washington Parish 34

ESTATE NAMES
  Bedford 21
  Belisle 53
  Berry Plain 21
  Buena Vista 21
  Cedar Grove 61
  Chestnut View 34
  Eagles' Nest 23, 37
  Eden 21
  Edgewood 4
  Fairhaven 61
  Gunston Hall 19
  Hastings Place 59
  Kenlock Farm 56
  Marmion 20, 21

Mount Chene 19
Mt Lebanon Farm 63
Mount Stuart 21
Mount View 62
Potomac View 63
Powhatan 17
Salisbury 61
Shellfield 22
Society Hill 63
Spy Hill 23, 58, 59
Waterloo 21
Willow Hill 30
Windsor 21, 23

www.ingramcontent.com/pod-product-compliance
Lightning Source LLC
Chambersburg PA
CBHW070256290326
41930CB00041B/2608